PIZZA

Also by Bruce Weinstein and Mark Scarbrough

The Ultimate Cook Book: 900 New Recipes, Thousands of Ideas

The Ultimate Peanut Butter Book

The Ultimate Frozen Dessert Book

The Ultimate Chocolate Cookie Book

The Ultimate Muffin Book

Cooking for Two: 125 Recipes for Every Day and Those Special Nights

The Ultimate Potato Book

The Ultimate Brownie Book

The Ultimate Shrimp Book

The Ultimate Candy Book

The Ultimate Party Drink Book

The Ultimate Ice Cream Book

Grill It, Bake It, Love It!

PIZZA

Bruce Weinstein AND Mark Scarbrough

with Photographs by Lucy Schaeffer

wm

WILLIAM MORROW
An Imprint of HarperCollinsPublishers

HarperCollins books may be purchased for educational, business, or sales promotional use. For information please write: Special Markets Department, HarperCollins Publishers, 10 East 53rd Street, New York, NY 10022.

FIRST EDITION

Designed by Jessica Shatan Heslin/Studio Shatan, Inc.

Library of Congress Cataloging-in-Publication Data has been applied for.

ISBN 978-0-06-143445-7

10   11   12   13   WBC/QW   10   9   8   7   6   5   4   3   2

Contents

PIZZA

Introduction

Of all the cookbooks we've written, this may be the most personal. We cook a lot during the week while recipe testing and tasting. Sundays are usually our time off. Personal time, as it were.

You'd think we'd eat out. But no, we fire up the grill or heat up the oven—because Sunday night is pizza night. Neighbors and friends in our part of northwestern Connecticut know the drill: there are hot pies to be had around 6:00 P.M.

We're clearly not alone. On average, each American eats more than 46 slices a year, much admittedly from one of the over 62,000 pizzerias across the country. And apparently in the dead of winter, too! More pizza is consumed in January than any other month—thanks mostly to the Super Bowl.

While a lot of that zealous consumption consists of frozen and takeout pies, homemade pizza is still the gold standard. It's fresher, more flavorful. The ingredients didn't sit around all day. The spices aren't tasteless. What's more, with homemade pizza, you can top it any way you want.

So here are our favorites, a good selection of what our neighbors and friends have come to love, just about every pizza imaginable—from the Italian-American classics to modern pies, from appetizer pizzas to full-on, well-stocked deep-dish belly-busters. Along the way, we'll also help you figure out your own choices by sometimes listing several options for one ingredient—for example, "2 ounces Parmigiano-Reggiano, or Grana Padano, or aged Asiago, finely grated"; or "2 tablespoons minced parsley, or oregano, or rosemary, or a combination of any two." This way, you can twist the flavors to suit your taste. After all, what's life without variation?

There's not much else to making a great pizza. Start with a good dough, either one you make yourself or one you've picked fresh from a pizza parlor or supermarket. Top it with fresh, flavorful ingredients. Don't skimp on the vegetables. And remember to let the pizza sit for five minutes once out of the oven so a too-hot slice doesn't peel off the roof of your mouth.

And as for leftovers? Well, is there a better breakfast?

The Road Map for Pizza

Consider this a general guide to everything that follows.

1. Choose how you want to cook the pie: on the grill (page 13) or in the oven (page 15).

2. Get your crust together, whether made from a fresh dough or a purchased prebaked crust. Fresh doughs can either be homemade or bought at the store (page 19). If using a fresh dough, either shape it on a pizza peel (page 20) or else press it into form on a pizza tray or a large baking sheet (page 21).

3. Create the topping for the pie you've selected.

4. If the pie has been made on a pizza peel, slip it carefully onto the preheated pizza stone either on the grill or in the oven. If the pie has been made on a pizza tray or a baking sheet, simply place the pie on its sheet on the unheated portion of the grill or right in the oven.

5. Cook the pizza until it's done.

6. If you're working with a stone, slip the peel back under the pie to take it off the grill or out of the oven. Then gently transfer the cooked pie to a wire rack to cool completely. If you're working with a pizza tray or baking sheet, transfer that tray to a wire rack to cool a minute or two, then slip the pie off the tray and onto the wire rack on its own. A pie that sits on a tray will steam and turn gummy.

7. Slice the pizza into wedges or sections to serve.

8. Pizza leftovers are heaven attained, but not by faith alone. Cool the pie completely, then place it on a plate and cover loosely with wax paper. A tight seal can lead to a gummy crust. Leftover pizza from a restaurant is always perfect because it sits in that box with lots of air space around the pie, so that the crust dries out a bit before it turns soggy.

Tools

Besides the usual—knives, cutting boards, rubber spatulas, and the like—pizza making calls for a few specialty tools.

Pizza stone. Although not necessary for pizza making, this large block of stone, ceramic, or synthetic material assures a crisp crust every time. A flat stone gets very hot, sort of like a griddle. It thus replicates a professional pizza oven in your home: the dough lies right on the heated surface of the stone the same way it sits on the floor of a pizza oven. If you don't use a stone, form the crust on a large baking sheet—see page 21.

As a general rule, buy the largest stone that will fit comfortably on your grill rack and/or in your oven. It's almost impossible to make a 13-inch pizza fit on a 13-inch stone without the pizza itself slipping and dripping off the edge.

The stone must be preheated for 30 to 45 minutes to ensure that it's hot enough to cook the crust from the bottom up. If a room-temperature stone is placed in a hot oven or on a grill, that stone may crack. To avoid this catastrophe, place the stone on the unheated section of the grill rack or on the oven rack positioned in the middle of the oven the moment you begin preheating either.

Never place the stone directly over the heat source on the grill. Grill heat is much hotter than oven heat; direct heat can fracture a stone.

A pizza stone will get browned and stained over time. Since it's porous, it will absorb almost any food that gets on it—melted cheese, olive oil, burned bits of flour, pepperoni grease. That said, never clean it with soap or other cleaning products. These will get into the pores, only to come back out and onto the crust the next time the stone is heated. Instead, scrape off any browned material while the stone is still hot, then cool the stone before you wipe the stone with a damp paper towel. The stone will sanitize over the intense heat the next time it's used.

If you don't want to go to the expense of buying a pizza stone, you can buy inexpensive, unglazed ceramic tiles at most home remodeling stores or almost all tile stores. Look for flat but thick tiles that fit tightly together—uneven seams can make it difficult to get the pizza on and off them with the peel (see below). Set the tiles tightly against each other on the unheated grill or oven rack, but do not line them up all the way to the sides of your oven. Air must circulate; leave at least two inches of open space around the tiles so heat can rise and move freely in the oven.

Pizza tray. This round baking sheet holds a pie in the oven or on the grill rack without the need for a stone. Simply place the pie on its tray in the oven or over the unheated section of the grill grate. That said, a large, heavy-duty, rectangular, lipped baking sheet will work just as well. No, the pizza will not be round, but the final result will be just as satisfying.

Pizza screen. This wire-mesh, round screen sits right on a pizza stone and lifts the pie an inch or so off the hot surface so that the crust crisps evenly. You'll end up with a more crackerlike crust: less bready and crunchier.

We don't use a pizza screen, preferring instead all those dark blotches across the crust's bottom, the charred bits you can only get if the crust sits directly on a hot surface. Also, a pizza screen can be tricky to work with—getting the topped pie from the peel to the stone and back off again.

Still, if you like crunchy crusts, invest in a screen. Lay the stretched dough on top of a well-oiled screen, build the toppings, then set the pizza on its screen on the peel (see below), and transfer it to the stone. When done, slip the peel back under the screen if a pizza stone is used, thereby removing the screen and the pie together.

The tricky part is then getting the pizza itself off the screen. Sometimes, you can bend the pie up in one section, get a good grip, and get the thing off the screen in one piece with a smooth pull. If the dough has slipped down through the cracks in the screen or fused to it in any way, cut the pizza into wedges and attempt to pry them off the screen one by one.

Pizza peel. This wooden paddle is designed to get the topped pie onto and off a pizza stone, so it is only necessary if the pie is indeed being baked on a stone. A peel should have a long handle to keep your hands out of the heat. It should also be sturdy but lightweight, with a tapered edge so you can slip it under a baked pie to take it off the stone.

It's not necessary to wash a peel; water warps its wood. If you're careful, you should never have to do anything except wipe it off with a clean kitchen towel. To avoid spills, don't use it as a cutting board and don't serve a pizza right off the peel. Transfer the baked pie to a cutting board or a sturdy, knife-safe platter before slicing and serving. If you must wash the peel, avoid soap and dry it thoroughly and carefully, letting it continue to dry on its edge, never flat (one side can remain damp and then warp). Never put a peel in the dishwasher.

Pizza wheel. Sometimes called a "pizza cutter," this round blade rolls through the pie to cut it into wedges without shredding the toppings. To make sure the wheel works well, look for one with a large diameter so that the toppings on the pie stay intact during cutting. Some wheels have a guard or protector over part of the sharp wheel. It's a nice safety feature but can get caught in the toppings, pulling them this way and that.

Deep-dish pizza pan. These specialty pans are not standardized; there is no one size that is the accepted depth, width, and height. Because of that, we do not call for any deep-dish pans. Instead, all the deep-dish pies were tested in a

10-inch cake pan with 2-inch-high sides—a standardized pan size to ensure you get the same results we did.

Oil the pan generously. And keep this in mind: a dark cake pan will yield a more darkly colored crust.

Do not use a nonstick cake pan; it will get nicked and scratched as you try to remove the pizza.

Cheese

Hard, semihard, and semisoft cheeses should be bought in blocks, rounds, or wedges and grated just before using. Pregrated and preshredded cheeses are time-savers, although some do not have much taste and are simply shaped oil masquerading as cheese.

There are three ways the cheese can be prepared for these recipes:

1. Shredded. Use a box grater, shredding the cheese through the large holes—or a hand grater with holes about the same size as the large ones on a box grater. Never shred cheese hours before using it; shredded cheese loses too much moisture if it sits around for more than 30 minutes. Of course, you'll rarely find the exact amount of cheese you need at the grocery store—say, 3 ounces of Cheddar. If you want to be precise, buy a large chunk and use the kitchen scales to determine when you've shredded the right amount. Set a small bowl on the scales, adjust the weighing mechanism so it zeroes out with the bowl in place (the "tare" on most automatic scales), and then shred the cheese into the bowl. Or find out how much the block of cheese weighs up front (8 ounces, for example), then shred off some cheese, weighing the block occasionally until you get as much shaved off as you need, doing the math by subtraction. For example, if you need 3 ounces, there should be a 5-ounce piece of the 8-ounce block left when you're done. As a third alternative, use the shredding blade of a food processor. You'll need to weigh the piece first and feed as much into the tube as you need. All that said, a pizza is not as exacting as some fancy French dessert. A little more cheese—it can hardly hurt. You can eyeball amounts and still come up with a great pie.

2. Finely grated. Hard cheeses—like Parmigiano-Reggiano or aged Asiago—can be grated into much thinner threads. To do so, use the small holes of a box grater or a small-holed Microplane, a culinary device specifically designed for hard cheeses. Since you need to grate all the cheese finely without leaving little balls and lumps that can result from that last bit slipping over the grates (not to mention peeling skin off your fingers), it helps to buy more cheese than you'll need, then grate only a portion of the block. If desired, use a kitchen scale so you make sure you've grated the right amount.

3. Shaved into thin strips. Hard cheeses can also be cut into paper-thin strips, using a vegetable peeler or a cheese plane, a specialty tool that passes over the block and shaves off a thin strip through a long slit in the plane. You can also use a mandoline, a specialty kitchen tool with a razor-sharp blade; but the effort of working with (and washing) a mandoline and grip seems to rule out the point. Failing a cheese plane, you can use the shaving blade on the side of some box graters—or the 1mm slicing blade in some food processors.

Pizza is not just a layer of mozzarella under other toppings. The best pies are made with a variety of cheeses. Here are the cheeses used in this book.

Asiago. Originally made near Venice but now made across North America, this cow's milk cheese has a taste reminiscent of creamy Cheddar but is sometimes used as a substitute for Pecorino or other hard cheeses. There are now hundreds of types of Asiago: from the fresh, oily Asiago *pressato* to dry and crumbly Asiago *d'allevo*. For pizza making, seek out drier versions; they're better for grating. Wetter, softer versions of Asiago can melt too quickly and run across the pie.

Brie. Originally a French cheese, named for its eponymous region, this soft, cow's milk cheese is now made in several locations across North America. The creamy cheese is encased in an edible white rind. For pizza making, however, the rind should be removed so that the soft inner cheese can be spread on the crust. While the cheese is still cold, slice off the top rind with a knife; then set the cheese aside to come to room temperature for several hours before scooping out and spreading the runny cheese with a rubber spatula.

Cheddar. Although true Cheddar is the most popular cheese in the United Kingdom, accounting for more than 50 percent of the nation's total cheese consumption, this white, grainy, aged cheese is a rarity in the United States, where it has been replaced by the familiar orange block, sold in a taste spectrum of "mild," "medium," "sharp," and "extra-sharp." Indeed, it is this American variety that is called for in this book. For the best taste, use a medium-flavored Cheddar.

Danish blue. Also known as "Danablu," this aged, creamy, blue cheese was originally developed in Denmark by cheesemaker Marius Boel as competition for French Roquefort (see page 13). Danish blue is perhaps the mildest of the blue cheeses commonly found in supermarkets—and also the saltiest. It is spreadable if left at room temperature for 3 or 4 hours.

Edam. This pale, mild, slightly sweet cheese is sometimes used as a substitute for Emmental, Cheddar, Gouda, or even Gruyère. It is far milder in taste than any of these, offering a slightly nutty aftertaste. It is also often softer than those other cheeses, primarily due to its lower fat content.

Emmental. Also called "Emmentaler," "Emmenthal," or "Emmenthaler," this mild, semifirm cow's milk cheese with its characteristic holes is probably the original Swiss cheese. Little of it is now made in Switzerland except high-end, aged varieties that would be great for a cheese plate but inappropriate on pizza. Most commercial Emmental suitable for pizza is made elsewhere—or subcontracted out by Swiss firms.

Feta. Made from goat's, sheep's, and/or cow's milk, this Greek cheese is actually a form of cheese curd, rather than a fully formed block of cheese. It is crumbly, white, and slightly sour, although its flavor can vary widely depending on the cheese's quality, acid content, and age. It's best stored in brine or a whey mixture because it dries out quickly at room temperature. Buy the block and store it in your refrigerator in its brine or whey solution for up to 3 months.

Fontina. This moderately high-fat cow's milk cheese from Italy comes in several varieties, from a soft cheese reminiscent of Taleggio or Brie to a hard cheese that can be grated like Parmigiano-Reggiano. Use a moderately firm version for the pizzas in this book. Look for the name "FONTINA" stamped on the rind along with a picture of the Matterhorn.

Goat cheese. Often called *chèvre,* French for "goat," there are hundreds of varieties on the market—some aged and hard, some fresh and soft. In standard North American cooking parlance, "goat cheese" refers to a soft cheese, often sold in small, cylinder-shaped pieces, sometimes under the brand name "Montrachet," a section of Burgundy, France. Although goat cheese is sometimes herbed or peppered, buy only the fresh plain, creamy variety for pizza making.

Gorgonzola. This Italian blue cheese is made by lacing the cow's milk with a strain of penicillin, then inserting metal rods into the formed cheese to create holes into which the blue mold can bloom during aging. Gorgonzola actually comes in several varieties: soft, aged (and thus firm), and even a sweetened version, sometimes used for dessert. Use the soft version for these pizzas; it should have the texture of Camembert or room-temperature Brie.

Gouda. Again not one thing but many, this pale yellow, mild, cow's milk cheese originally from the Netherlands is made by washing the curd with water to remove some of the lactic acid, thereby producing a sweeter cheese. The orange, rubbery varieties, often sold under the same name in the United States, are knock-off imitators. That said, they are perfectly acceptable on a pie if they are the bottom cheese, the one on which the other ingredients sit. These knockoffs are less acceptable as the top cheese because of their too mild taste and oily-when-melted texture. Aged Gouda, like Boerenkaas, is a specialty best saved for a cheese plate.

Grana Padano. Like Parmigiano-Reggiano (see page 11), Grana Padano is an Italian cheese made in large, cylindrical wheels from partly skimmed cow's milk. It has a grainy texture (thus, *grana* in Italian; "Padano" refers to the region around the Po River). Compared with Parmigiano-Reggiano, Grana Padano is slightly sweeter and definitely milder, perhaps a better choice when kids are going to have part of the pie. The name should be clearly stamped on the hard rind.

Gruyère. This pale, hard, mild, salty Swiss cheese is made from partially cooked cow's milk. It is the cheese used atop French onion soup; it is also a favorite in all sorts of cooking because it complements, rather than overpowers, other flavors. Although available in a wide variety, Gruyère is usually sold in the U.S. in two versions: mild (sometimes labeled *doux*—French for "sweet"), which has been aged for 5 months or less, and *réserve*, a little stronger and aged for up to 10 months. Either will do for these pizzas, although the mild/*doux* is more economical.

Havarti. This buttery, semisoft, rindless Danish cheese turns quite soft if left at room temperature for an hour or so. Although aged versions exist, it's best for pizzas in its soft, creamy, young state.

Jarlsberg. Often thought of as a Norwegian version of Emmental (see page 8), Jarlsberg is nonetheless more buttery, somewhat more pliable, and definitely sweeter. Made from cow's milk, the cheese has an inedible rind and a characteristic, waxy sheen. In the late 1980s, a so-called "light" version was developed, one with less of that characteristic butteriness but also (of course) somewhat less fat. Either is good for the pizzas in this book.

Manchego. This mild, nutty, pale white or pale yellow sheep's milk cheese from Spain is available in three forms: *fresco* (fresh, like fresh mozzarella), *curado* (aged 3 to 6 months), and *viejo* (aged at least 1 year). Only the latter two are acceptable for these pizzas—and curado is less expensive than viejo, which is best reserved for eating on its own. Look for a semifirm cheese, not quite as hard as Parmigiano-Reggiano but certainly shreddable, even gratable. The rind is inedible.

Monterey Jack. Franciscan monks in Monterey, California, once made this white cheese. It received its current name from its first promoter and marketer, David Jack, and was originally called "Jack's cheese." It is quite mild, best used in cooking where its fat content carries other flavors. For these pies, do not use any flavored Jack cheese (pepper Jack, etc.) or any aged Jack, hard like Pecorino and best for grating over salads.

Montrachet. See Goat cheese. Montrachet is a branded version of one form of soft goat cheese.

Mozzarella. The classic pizza cheese bears little resemblance to fresh mozzarella. This is a semihard, waxy, grating cheese, often used as the bottom cheese on pizzas, the cheese on which everything else lies. It allows the flavors of the other ingredients to be more present, thanks to its mild flavor and moderately high fat content. It is often sold pregrated—check the label to make sure you're buying cheese, not an imitation product.

Fresh mozzarella, by contrast, is a pure white, mild cheese, usually formed, sold, and consumed on the same day. Buffalo mozzarella (*mozzarella di bufala*) is made from the milk of a certain type of water buffalo; other fresh mozzarella is made from cow's milk. The cheese maker stretches and shapes the cheese, about like kneading bread, and then cuts off sections for sale. Fresh mozzarella is sometimes available in a brine bath at the supermarket salad bar—but beware: that brine can turn it untenably rubbery and salty. Instead, search out fresh mozzarella at small Italian markets or better-quality cheese counters at supermarkets.

Muenster. American Muenster is a pale yellow, semisoft cheese, quite creamy, with an orange rind. It bears little resemblance to brine-washed Alsatian Munster, which is white with a thin, Brielike rind and a musky taste. American Muenster is better for pizzas because it melts smoothly and has a less complex taste, a better foil to the other toppings. If yours is too soft to grate, place it in the freezer for up to 3 hours so it will firm up just slightly.

Parmigiano-Reggiano. This hard, skimmed cow's milk Italian cheese is most often finely grated with a Microplane or shaved into strips with a cheese plane. Buy small chunks that have been cut off larger wheels; these chunks should have as little rind as possible to cut down on waste. The rind should be stamped with the cheese's name and origin for authenticity.

Pecorino. This is the name for an entire group of Italian sheep's milk cheeses, almost all quite hard like Parmigiano-Reggiano but with a stronger, sharper, and saltier taste. The name "Pecorino" is usually paired with a second word to indicate the place of origin—for example, Pecorino Romano ("Roman Pecorino," which these days is mostly made in Sardinia or Tuscany).

Provolone. This Italian, aged, semihard cow's milk cheese originated in southern Italy but is now made almost exclusively in the northern part of the country. It has a slightly stronger, more pungent taste than standard mozzarella, for which it is often a substitute to go with more fiery or herbaceous tomato sauces. There are multiple varieties from the very sharp *piccante* to the sweet *dolce*. A less flavored, more neutral provolone is better for pizza.

Queso blanco. This soft Mexican cheese is made by pressing the whey from cottage cheese, making it similar to farmer cheese. Queso blanco is white and lacks any rind. It is most often crumbled onto pizzas like feta.

Raclette. This semifirm, salty, creamy cheese originated in Switzerland but is now almost exclusively associated with a dish served in the French Alps on either side of the border, a dish of potatoes and melted cheese to which the cheese gives its name. Raclette melts exceptionally well; remove the rind before using on pizza.

Ricotta. Ricotta is made from whey, an often discarded by-product of cheese making. It's sort of like cottage cheese but creamier. Because it is made from whey, rather than milk itself, there can be regular, low-fat, and even fat-free versions of ricotta. As a health note, fat-free versions will work here in deep-dish pies but will turn too runny when placed on a standard crust.

Ricotta salata. This is a dried, salted, and pressed version of ricotta, often sold in cones. It can be grated like Parmigiano-Reggiano or Pecorino; in fact, it is most often a milder, sweeter substitute for these cheeses.

Roquefort. This blue cheese is made from sheep's milk, not cow's, and is renowned for its pungent, stinky, sour taste. Originally, it was made in certain French caves that were hosts to naturally occurring penicillin colonies. Bread was left in the caves for 6 to 8 weeks to mold and be almost fully consumed by the bacilli; the resulting mass was dried, ground, and bored into the cheese wheels to produce the characteristic blue mottling. The process today is much simpler; the result, a little less complex but still quite odoriferous.

Soy mozzarella. Soy cheese is made by forming soy curds (much like tofu) into blocks (much like cheese). There are sometimes additions of artificial or natural flavors. Soy cheese will not melt like milk cheese; it has a more plastic, rubbery texture. That said, soy cheese is an acceptable substitute for dairy cheese if the soy cheese is put under other ingredients on the pie where their naturally re-leased moisture will improve its texture dramatically.

Swiss. This generic name is given to any white to pale yellow, shiny cheese with holes. A knockoff of Emmental (see page 8), Swiss is certainly an economical if less tasty substitute.

Pizzas on the Grill

The grill's high-intensity heat sears the crust, melts the cheese, and creates the best all-around pizza—mostly because a grill efficiently replicates the high-heat, low-moisture environment of commercial pizza ovens.
There are two ways to grill a pizza:

1. **On a pizza stone** (see page 3). A stone is placed over indirect, moderate (or medium) heat; the topped pie is then placed directly on the stone and cooked with the grill lid closed.

2. On the grate. The formed but not-yet-topped crust is laid directly on the grate and (most important) over low—not medium or high—heat. It is grilled for 2 minutes, then flipped to be topped right on the grill. The pie continues to bake another 5 to 8 minutes; the exact timing depends on how many toppings have been added.

We advocate for the first option. First off, you can load a pizza more thickly with toppings when you bake it on a stone because they have time to heat through and meld. In other words, using a stone lets you use more cheese. It seems like a no-brainer.

Secondly, there's little chance of burning the crust. A low-heat setting can be difficult to maintain in a charcoal grill and the crust will burn quite quickly if the heat inches up even slightly.

Since we advocate for the stone over indirect heat, these pies are technically barbecued, not grilled. In culinary parlance, grilling is when you cook something directly over the heat; barbecuing is when you cook the food to the side of the heat source—that is, indirectly.

One caveat: a stone must be preheated 30 to 45 minutes. A cool stone will lead to a soggy, underdone crust and burned toppings. Do not shortchange this step.

Indirect cooking on a gas grill: First set up the grill for moderate (or medium) heat, which runs about 450°F. On a gas grill, this is no problem: set the dial and watch the temperature gauge. If you don't have a gauge, buy an oven thermometer and hang it inside the grill to get an accurate reading.

Heat only half of the grill—back or front; one side or the other. Unless you have a large grill, it's almost impossible to heat an area that will be completely separate from your pizza stone (or its substitute, a large baking tray—see page 21). If there is some overlap between the heat source and the stone or the tray, make sure that overlap occurs at the side of the stone or tray. If your burners run front to back, turn the top and bottom burners to medium and let the grill heat up for 30 to 40 minutes with the lid closed. The stone or the baking tray should be set so that its center is over the unheated center burner of the grill. If your burners run side to side, turn on only those at one side, setting the stone or the baking sheet on the other side, the unheated section of the grill grate.

In any event, if there's overlap between the burner and the stone or baking sheet, consider rotating the pizza halfway through baking to ensure it gets done evenly. On a baking sheet or pizza tray, this is no problem—just rotate the sheet or tray. On a stone, work with the peel, getting the firmed up if still underbaked pizza onto it and gently turning the pizza 90 degrees before again placing it over on the stone and closing the lid.

Indirect cooking on a charcoal grill: Since you'll need to have the heat to the side of the pizza stone, you must either build the coal bed along the outside edge or perimeter of the coal rack with quick-lighting charcoal, or you must build a coal bed in the center of the rack and then rake those hot, red, ashed coals to the rack's perimeter so the stone can sit in the center of the upper grill rack without any direct heat under it. If you use a chimney, make sure the vents are partially open so the coals become quite hot but gray with ash. Once the coals are in place for indirect cooking, place the stone in the center of the grill (again, not directly over the heat source). Because the stone must heat for 30 to 45 minutes, have more coals at the ready, adding them two or three at a time to keep the heat constant.

Preheating a charcoal grill is a less exact science than doing the same for a gas grill. Moderate heat means that you can hold your hand about 6 inches above the coals for about 4 seconds before you must move it for fear of getting burned. Of course, you can also buy an oven thermometer and hang it off the upper grill rack to determine the exact temperature. Again, moderate heat should register about 450°F.

Pizzas in the Oven

Baking a pizza is a matter of heating the stone, if you've used one, and then watching to make sure the cheese melts properly and the crust browns at its edges. Of course, baking a pizza on a baking sheet in the oven is hardly different from baking a tray of cookies. Still, there are three tips for success:

1. Position the rack in the center of the oven. Too close to the bottom and the crust will burn before the cheese melts or the topping cooks through. Too close to the top and the pizza will never get done.

2. The oven can turn a pie a little doughy, a little bready. Compensate by rolling and pressing the crust a little thinner than you would for the grill.

3. Treat the baking times as suggestions. Don't just set a timer and walk away. Pay careful attention to how the crust is browning, how the cheese is melting.

THE BASICS: EIGHT CRUSTS AND THREE SAUCES

Ahomemade crust is a beautiful thing. Yes, excellent doughs and crusts are available at supermarkets—and we certainly use them when we are pressed for time. But a crust from scratch is a pleasure, something to savor on slow Sunday, weekend, or holiday afternoons.

Although most of these crusts are good basics, three are rather esoteric: the spelt, cracker, and gluten-free pizza doughs. These are specialty items that require a bit more work and cannot be shaped in the same way as traditional doughs. Follow the recipe for these exactly, using the technique for shaping them as stated here, not as stated for traditional doughs in the pizza recipes to follow. Top them and bake them, however, just as you would any pie.

As for these three basic sauces, each recipe will make more than you need for a pie. But if you're going to make sauce, you might as well make extra and freeze it for the next time.

Working with a Crust

When it comes to crusts, there are three choices:

1. Make a fresh dough at home.

2. Buy a fresh dough at the grocery store or a pizza parlor.

3. Buy a prebaked crust at the grocery store.

Working with Fresh Dough

First, a little matter of timing: if you're making a homemade dough from scratch, start making the dough an hour and a half or so before you want to eat so the dough can rise in a warm, draft-free place.

That said, you don't need to make fresh dough. Walk into almost any pizza parlor and ask for the dough for a small pie. They'll sell you one for a few bucks.

Or use store-bought dough at the supermarket, often available near the fresh pasta or in the dairy case. These doughs vary in taste and quality. Some are fat-free, made only with flour, yeast, and water; others have oil or hydrogenated shortening in the mix. Read the labels carefully to get the kind you want—but remember that these recipes call for 1 pound of dough.

Store-bought dough should be left at room temperature for 1 hour before using. If the dough is cold, it may tear when shaped.

"Fresh" doughs can also be frozen, and so, of course, are available in the freezer case at your supermarket. These must be thawed before they can be shaped and formed. Leave the dough in the refrigerator for 24 hours, then set it out at room temperature for 1 hour before shaping.

Once the dough is in your hands, it must be shaped for the pie. Here, you must make a decision: will you be using a peel and a pizza stone or will you be using a pizza tray or its substitute, a large baking sheet?

Fresh Dough on a Peel

Dust the peel with flour or cornmeal to keep the dough from sticking.

Place the dough on the peel and dimple it with your fingertips, pressing the dough out from the center, slowly widening the diameter as you continue to dimple its surface.

Pick up the dough by one edge, one hand at about ten o'clock and the other at about two. Hold the dough up so the flat (that is, nondimpled) side faces you, then turn the dough by its edge, stretching it slightly at its edge with your hands as you turn it but keeping your hands mostly in the ten and two positions as they make their way around the dough, thereby letting gravity pull the circle down as you gently stretch the edge, until the dough's a circle about 14 inches in diameter. In general, keep the edge a little thicker so there's a defined rim.

If a tear forms on the dough while it's being shaped, the dough probably cannot be pinched back together without help. Pizza doughs are too dry, too full of glutens, simply to stick together the way, say, a pie crust will. Use a little vegetable oil to seal the tear by swabbing its edges and pressing them together.

To get dough from the peel to the hot pizza stone, make sure it's not stuck to the peel. Before you add the toppings to the crust, shake the peel to make sure the dough moves around easily. If it doesn't, add more flour or cornmeal so the crust slides while on the peel. Once the crust is topped, shake the peel again—gently this time—to make sure the crust is still movable. Yes, some of the toppings may slip off the crust. But it's better to rearrange the toppings now than to have a pizza stuck on the peel.

To get the pizza onto the stone, position the peel at the back of the stone, shake the peel a little to get the pizza moving, then shake it again and pull the peel toward you until the back edge of the pizza is in contact with the stone. Continue to shake it as you pull the peel out, leaving the dough behind on the stone.

To get the cooked pizza back onto the peel, it's sometimes helpful to use tongs or a long-handled barbecue fork to hold the pizza crust so that the peel slides under the pie without its moving too far back on the stone. Slip the peel under the pie and take it off the stone.

Finally, to keep the crust from steaming and becoming soggy as it rests, slip it from the peel to a wire rack for cooling. Wait for 5 minutes and transfer it from the rack to a cutting board to slice it into wedges. It's an extra step that involves moving and switching but it assures a crisp crust every time.

Fresh Dough on a Pizza Tray or a Large Baking Sheet

Lightly grease the tray or sheet, using either oil dabbed on a paper towel or non-stick spray.

Place the dough on the tray or baking sheet, then dimple the dough from the center out, creating a round or oblong form, depending on whether you've used a round pizza tray or a rectangular baking sheet.

Next, grip the edge with one hand and use the heel of your other hand to stretch the dough to fit the sheet, either a round crust for a pizza tray or a rectangular if irregular, oblong one for a baking sheet. In any event, the dough will be slightly more irregular than one stretched by hand for a peel. The rim of the crust should be a little thicker than the center to help hold the toppings in place. If the dough should tear while it's on the tray or sheet, rub a little flour over the oiled surface and pinch the pieces together.

Place the tray or sheet either on the unheated section of the grill or in the oven and bake as the recipe indicates. Transfer the baking sheet to a wire rack to cool for a few minutes. If you want a crisper crust, remove the pie from the tray or sheet after a couple of minutes, transferring it directly to the wire rack. It can be a little tricky getting the pizza up over the baking sheet's lip. Lift up the edge of the crust and drag it off the baking sheet and onto the wire rack, lifting the sheet up to help the pie slide off.

Working with a Prebaked Crust

Technically, prebaked crusts are par-baked—that is, partially baked. They're like an English muffin: gummy out of the bag but crisp once toasted.

A prebaked crust will work on a pizza peel and a hot stone, a pizza tray, or a baking sheet. In general, a prebaked crust will not stick to the peel or the tray, so there is no need to grease or oil any of the equipment. You may need to shave a minute or two off the cooking time, so watch carefully and don't let the crust burn.

Many prebaked crusts come with some cheese already baked onto the crust; a little more won't hurt anything. However, do not buy already-flavored crusts (rosemary and garlic crust, for example); those flavorings will compete with others in the toppings.

Classic Pizza Dough

This is the basic crust, one without a lot of folderol. No fat, either—to make room for lots of cheese! Bread flour is a high-gluten wheat flour with a little malted barley flour and either vitamin C or potassium bromate in the mix. The barley flour provides quick food for the yeast; the other addition helps keep the glutens elastic so they'll hold the air bubbles the yeast produces. Look for bread flour in the baking aisle of almost all supermarkets.

MAKES 1 POUND DOUGH

⅔ **cup lukewarm water (between 105°F and 115°F)**
1½ **teaspoons active dry yeast (see Note)**
½ **teaspoon sugar**
½ **teaspoon salt**
1 **cup bread flour**
1 **cup all-purpose flour, plus additional for dusting**
Vegetable oil or nonstick spray

1. A mixing bowl or the bowl to a stand mixer can often be quite cool—and thus a detriment to the yeast. If yours feels cool to the touch, fill it first with some warm tap water, drain it, and dry it thoroughly. Then stir the water, yeast, sugar, and salt together in the bowl just until everything is dissolved. Set aside at room temperature for 5 minutes to make sure the mixture bubbles and foams. If it doesn't, either the yeast expired or the water was not the right temperature. Throw the mixture out and start again.

2. *If working by hand:* Stir in both flours with a wooden spoon to make a soft dough. Sprinkle a clean, dry work surface with a light coating of all-purpose flour; turn the dough out onto it, and knead for 8 minutes by pulling the mass with one hand while twisting it with the other, all the while digging the heel of your twisting hand into the dough. After every two or three push/twist/dig actions, rearrange the dough by folding it onto itself. If the dough is sticking to your hands, add a little more all-purpose flour, no more than 1 tablespoon or so; then continue kneading until smooth and elastic, about 8 minutes.

If working with a stand mixer: Add both flours, attach the dough hook, and beat at medium speed until a soft dough forms. Continue beating, adding more all-purpose flour in 1-tablespoon increments if the dough gets sticky, until the mixture is soft and elastic, about 6 minutes.

3. Wipe a clean, large bowl with a bit of cooking oil on a paper towel; or spray it with nonstick spray. Place the dough in the prepared bowl, turning the dough so all sides are coated with oil, and cover the bowl with plastic wrap. Set aside in a warm, draft-free place until doubled in bulk, about 1½ hours. Shape the dough according to the instructions on page 20 or as directed in the individual pizza recipe.

NOTE: Active dry yeast can be stored in the freezer for up to 1 year to preserve its freshness.

Whole Wheat Pizza Dough

With more tooth and a little more flavor than the Classic Pizza Dough, this hearty dough stands up to heavier toppings like the Lamejun Pizza (page 142) or the Roasted Roots Pizza (page 246). Whole wheat dough, despite the heavier flour, is actually delicate and so may tear slightly when shaped. For easier handling, consider rolling it into the desired shape with a rolling pin. To do so, dimple the dough on the peel or the baking sheet, then roll it out to the desired size, dusting it lightly with all-purpose flour if the dough sticks to the pin.

MAKES 1 POUND DOUGH

¾ cup lukewarm water (between 105°F and 115°F)
2 teaspoons active dry yeast
1 teaspoon sugar
½ teaspoon salt
1⅓ cups whole wheat flour
⅔ cup all-purpose flour, plus additional as needed
2 tablespoons walnut or canola or vegetable oil, plus additional for greasing

1. Place the water in a large bowl or the bowl to a stand mixer. Stir in the yeast, sugar, and salt. Wait 5 minutes so the yeast can activate and begin to bubble and foam. If it does not, throw the mixture out and start again. Either the water wasn't the right temperature or the yeast expired.

2. *If working by hand:* Stir both flours and the oil into the yeast mixture until a soft dough forms. Lightly dust a clean, dry work surface with all-purpose flour and turn the dough onto it. Knead by holding the dough with one hand, stretching it with the other, and then twisting the heel of the holding hand into the mass. Continually reshape the dough, folding it on itself as you knead. If it's sticking to your hands, add a little more all-purpose flour in about 1 tablespoon increments. Continue kneading until smooth and elastic, about 10 minutes.

If working with a stand mixer: Attach the dough hook and the bowl to the mixer, add both flours and the oil to the bowl with the yeast, and stir at medium speed until combined. Continue kneading at medium speed until smooth and elastic, adding extra all-purpose flour in 1-tablespoon increments if the dough sticks, about 8 minutes.

3. Wipe a clean, large bowl with a bit of cooking oil on a paper towel; or spray it with nonstick spray. Place the dough in the prepared bowl, turning the dough so all sides are coated with oil, and cover the bowl with plastic wrap. Set aside in a warm, draft-free place until doubled in bulk, about 1½ hours. Shape the dough using the tips on page 20 or as directed in the individual pizza recipes.

Olive Oil Pizza Dough

Here's a dough that's more in keeping with some versions of pizza found in southern Italy and at Sicilian-style restaurants in North America. It produces a crisper, richer crust. For the best taste, use a fragrant, fruity olive oil.

MAKES 1 POUND DOUGH

½ cup lukewarm water (between 105°F and 115°F)
1½ teaspoons active dry yeast
½ teaspoon sugar
½ teaspoon salt
2 cups bread flour, plus additional as needed
¼ cup olive oil, plus additional for greasing the bowl

1. If the bowl you're using—either a mixing bowl or the one for a stand mixer—feels cool to the touch, fill it with warm tap water, drain it, and thoroughly dry it. Then stir the warm water, yeast, sugar, and salt in the bowl, just until the yeast dissolves. Set aside so the yeast can begin to bubble and foam, about 5 minutes. If it doesn't, throw the mixture out and start again. The water may not have been the right temperature or the yeast expired.

2. *If working by hand:* Stir in the flour and olive oil until fairly uniform, then turn the dough out onto a lightly floured, clean, dry work surface. Knead the dough until smooth and elastic, pulling it with one hand while digging into it with the heel of the other hand, repositioning the mass repeatedly and adding more bread flour in 1-tablespoon increments if sticky. The whole process should take about 8 minutes.

If working with a stand mixer: Add the flour and oil to the yeast mixture, attach the dough hook, and stir at medium speed until combined. Continue beating at medium speed for about 7 minutes, until smooth and elastic, adding a little more bread flour (say, a tablespoon or two) if the dough starts to crawl up the hook or get sticky.

3. Wipe a clean, large bowl with a bit of olive oil on a paper towel. Place the dough in the prepared bowl, turning the dough so all sides are coated with oil, and cover the bowl with plastic wrap. Set aside in a warm, draft-free place until doubled in bulk, about 2 hours. Shape the dough using the tips on page 20 or as directed in the individual pizza recipes.

Semolina Pizza Dough

Semolina flour is made from durum wheat, a very hard wheat, traditionally used in pasta making. It's somewhat granular, which is why cornmeal and even some rice flours ground to the same consistency are occasionally called semolina. Look for the real thing, the wheat flour, at specialty markets and Italian food stores. It will give the crust a nutty, full-bodied richness, perfect with pizzas that call for a tomato sauce.

MAKES 1 POUND DOUGH

¾ cup lukewarm water (between 105°F and 115°F)
1½ teaspoons active dry yeast
½ teaspoon sugar
¼ teaspoon salt
1½ cups all-purpose flour, plus additional as needed
½ cup semolina flour
2 tablespoons olive oil, plus additional for greasing the bowl

1. Pour the water in a slightly warmed, large bowl or the warmed bowl of a stand mixer. Stir in the yeast, sugar, and salt. Set aside until the yeast is bubbling and foamy, about 5 minutes. If the yeast does not indeed "proof," throw the mixture out—either the yeast expired or the water was too hot or too cold.

2. *If working by hand:* Stir both flours and the oil into the yeast mixture until fairly smooth. Lightly dust a clean, dry work surface with a little all-purpose flour, then turn the dough out onto it. Knead by hand, adding a tablespoon or two of additional all-purpose flour should the dough turn sticky. Pull the dough with one hand while digging and twisting the heel of the other hand into the mass, always repositioning the dough by folding it onto itself, working all the while, until it's smooth and elastic, about 8 minutes.

If working with a stand mixer: Add both flours and the oil to the yeast mixture, attach the dough hook, and stir at medium speed until fairly well combined.

Continue kneading at medium speed, adding a little extra flour if the dough should stick, until smooth and elastic, about 7 minutes.

3. Wipe a clean, large bowl with a bit of olive oil on a paper towel; or spray it with nonstick spray. Place the dough in the prepared bowl, turning the dough so all sides are coated with oil, and cover the bowl with plastic wrap. Set aside in a warm, draft-free place until doubled in bulk, about 1½ hours. Shape the dough using the tips on page 20 or as directed in the individual pizza recipes.

Parmesan Pizza Dough

This rich dough is best with simple toppings, like the Prosciutto and Arugula Pizza (page 242) or the Delicata Squash and Chard Pizza (page 212), because the flavor of the Parmesan will come through the crust. Use only good Parmigiano-Reggiano, purchased from a wheel at the market and grated just before using at home (see page 12 for more details).

MAKES 1 POUND DOUGH

¾ cup plus 1 tablespoon lukewarm water (between 105°F and 115°F)

1½ teaspoons active dry yeast

¼ teaspoon sugar

¼ teaspoon salt

2 cups all-purpose flour, plus additional as needed

2 ounces Parmigiano-Reggiano, finely grated

1 tablespoon olive oil, plus additional for greasing the bowl

1. Place the water in a slightly warmed, large bowl or the warmed bowl of a stand mixer. (To warm the bowl, just rinse it out with warm tap water before wiping it out.) Add the yeast, sugar, and salt. Stir well and set aside until the mixture begins to foam and get frothy, about 5 minutes. If for any reason it doesn't, throw it out and start again to assure a good crust.

2. *If working by hand:* Stir the flour, grated cheese, and olive oil into the yeast mixture until smooth. Dust a clean, dry work surface with a little flour and turn the dough out onto it. Knead by holding with one hand while pulling and twisting with the other, digging the heel of that twisting hand into the dough as you pull it. Continually reposition the dough and re-form it into a mass as you knead it, adding more all-purpose flour if the dough sticks to your hands. Keep kneading until the dough is smooth and elastic, about 8 minutes.

If working with a stand mixer: Add the flour, cheese, and oil to the yeast mixture, attach the dough hook, and stir at medium speed until fairly uniform.

Continue kneading at medium speed, adding a little more all-purpose flour should the dough turn sticky or climb up the hook, until smooth and elastic, about 7 minutes.

3. Wipe a clean, large bowl with a bit of olive oil on a paper towel, or spray it with nonstick spray. Place the dough in the prepared bowl, turning the dough so all sides are coated with oil, and cover the bowl with plastic wrap. Set aside in a warm, draft-free place until doubled in bulk, about 1½ hours. Shape the dough using the tips on page 20 or as directed in the individual pizza recipes.

Spelt Pizza Dough

Spelt is a whole grain wheat, made from an ancient forerunner of today's wheat and also quite high in protein. But all nutrition aside, it makes a chewy but still crisp crust, a good base for heavy cheese sauces. A little potato flour gives the dough some elasticity; a bit of honey imparts a bit of sweetness.

MAKES 1 POUND DOUGH

¾ cup lukewarm water (between 105°F and 115°F)
2 teaspoons honey
2 teaspoons active dry yeast
¼ teaspoon salt
1¾ cups plus 2 tablespoons spelt flour, plus additional as needed
2 tablespoons potato flour (see Note)
1 teaspoon olive oil, plus additional for greasing the bowl

1. Pour the water in a slightly warmed, large bowl or the warmed bowl of a stand mixer. Stir in the honey, yeast, and salt. Set aside until a little foamy and frothy, about 5 minutes. If the yeast does not "proof," toss the mixture out and start again—either the water was at the wrong temperature or the yeast expired.

2. *If working by hand:* Stir the spelt flour, potato flour, and olive oil into the yeast mixture until fairly smooth. Lightly flour a clean, dry work surface, then turn the dough out onto it. Knead by holding with one hand and twisting the dough with the other while pushing the heel of that hand into the mass. If the dough sticks to your hands or the work surface, add another tablespoon or so of spelt flour as you knead. Reposition the dough, gather it together, and repeat this kneading process until well blended, 2 to 3 minutes.

If working with a stand mixer: Add the spelt flour, potato flour, and oil to the yeast mixture, attach the dough hook, and knead at medium speed until well combined and uniform, about 3 minutes.

3. Wipe a clean, large bowl with a bit of olive oil on a paper towel, or spray it with nonstick spray. Place the dough in the prepared bowl, turning the dough so all sides are coated with oil, and cover the bowl with plastic wrap. Set aside in a warm, draft-free place until doubled in bulk, about 1½ hours. Shape the dough for a tray using the tips on page 20 or as directed in the individual pizza recipes. Because spelt flour lacks many of the glutens found in all-purpose or bread flour, this dough can be very difficult to shape by tossing and stretching. Instead, place it on a lightly floured peel or work surface, dust the top with spelt flour, and roll with a rolling pin to the desired shape.

NOTE: Don't confuse potato flour with potato starch. Potato flour is made from ground, dried potatoes and is available in the baking aisle of high-end markets and almost all health food stores.

Cracker Pizza Dough

Look no further for the thinnest, crunchiest crust, a true Italian specialty. This dough is different from the others; it cannot be stretched into a crust once it's risen. Instead, it must be rolled out on a lightly floured peel or work surface until paper thin. There's no need to use the dough hook on a stand mixer for this crust; kneading by hand is a snap because so little flour is used.

MAKES 1 POUND DOUGH

½ **cup lukewarm water (between 105°F and 115°F)**
¼ **teaspoon active dry yeast**
¼ **teaspoon baking soda**
¼ **teaspoon salt**
1½ **cups bread flour, plus additional as needed**
2 **teaspoons olive oil, plus additional for greasing the bowl**

1. Pour the water into a slightly warmed, large bowl or the slightly warmed bowl of a stand mixer. Stir in the yeast, baking soda, and salt until dissolved.

2. Stir in the flour and olive oil until smooth. Dust a clean, dry work surface with a little bread flour, then turn the dough out onto it. Knead by holding the dough with one hand and pulling it with the other hand, twisting and digging the heel of that second hand into the dough as you pull it. Add a little more flour if the dough sticks; continue kneading until smooth and elastic, about 4 minutes.

3. Wipe a clean, large bowl with a bit of cooking oil on a paper towel, or spray it with nonstick spray. Place the dough in the prepared bowl, turning the dough so all sides are coated with oil, and cover the bowl with plastic wrap. Set aside in a warm, draft-free place to rest for 2 hours. Because there's not much yeast, the dough will not double in bulk but will rise a little and soften somewhat. Roll the dough into the desired shape on a flour-dusted peel or work surface rather than tossing it by hand.

Gluten-Free Pizza Dough

Even if you don't have gluten allergies, try this specialty crust, made with instant masa mix, often used to make tamales and available in almost all supermarkets, often in the Mexican products aisle. The rice and potato flours are available at health food stores and high-end markets. The dough will not rise the way a yeast dough will. It will also not stretch because of the lack of wheat glutens, so you have to roll it out. We add a little gluten-free yeast to the mix, just for flavor.

MAKES 1 POUND DOUGH

1 cup lukewarm water (between 105°F and 115°F)
2 teaspoons sugar
1½ teaspoons gluten-free active dry yeast (see Note)
½ teaspoon salt
½ cup instant corn masa mix, plus additional for rolling out the dough and dusting a pizza peel
½ cup rice flour
½ cup potato flour (do not use potato starch)

1. Place the water in a large bowl; sprinkle the sugar, yeast, and salt on top. Stir until dissolved and set aside for 5 minutes so the yeast can begin to foam.

2. Mix the masa mix, rice flour, and potato flour in a second bowl until well blended.

3. Stir the flour mixture into the yeast mixture until it forms a ball. Should the mixture be too dry (the moisture content of masa mixes can fluctuate dramatically based on external humidity and temperature), add more water in 1-tablespoon increments until the whole mixture can be formed into a ball. Cover and set aside at room temperature for 20 minutes.

4. Dust a pizza peel with masa mix or grease a pizza tray or a large, rimless baking sheet with nonstick spray. Set the dough at the center of any of these, dust the dough with a little instant masa mix, and roll with a rolling pin to a 12- to 14-inch circle. If the edges crack, push them together to form a perfect circle. If desired, fold the edge over to form a lip on the crust. Top and bake as the recipe requires.

NOTE: Many packaged yeast varieties include various wheat glutens adhering to the yeast granules, both for storage and for better activation. You can find gluten-free yeast at health food stores.

Classic Pizza Sauce

This recipe makes enough sauce for about five pies, because who wants to go to the trouble of making just a small amount for one pizza? Freeze any leftover sauce in ½-cup plastic containers or zippered plastic bags for up to 3 months; thaw in the microwave on low or in the refrigerator overnight. Although onions are sometimes traditional in pizza sauce, this recipe omits them because they make the sauce too sweet. Besides, onions are best as a pie topping.

MAKES ABOUT 2¾ CUPS

One 28-ounce can reduced-sodium crushed tomatoes (see Note)
3 tablespoons olive oil
1 tablespoon sugar
2 teaspoons dried basil
1 teaspoon dried oregano
½ teaspoon salt
Up to ½ teaspoon red pepper flakes, optional
1 garlic clove, minced

1. Mix the tomatoes, olive oil, sugar, basil, oregano, salt, red pepper flakes (if using), and garlic in a large saucepan set over medium-high heat. Bring to a simmer, stirring occasionally.

2. Set the lid askew, reduce the heat to low, and simmer slowly, stirring occasionally, until the tomatoes have broken down into a somewhat thickened sauce, about 30 minutes. Cool for 10 minutes before using, or store, covered, in a plastic container in the refrigerator for up to 3 days. The best way to get sauce on a stretched dough is to use a ladle; spoon the sauce into the middle of the crust, then use the back of the ladle to spread the sauce evenly over the crust.

NOTE: The quality of the tomatoes will directly affect the quality of the sauce. Do a taste test sometime to discover a brand with true tomato taste without too much salt or acid.

No-Cook Pizza Sauce

Here's a real time-saver. Put everything in the blender or food processor and you've got pizza sauce in minutes. The basic flavors are pumped up with fresh basil leaves because the tomatoes never break down into their aromatic fullness as they would over the heat.

MAKES ABOUT 2⅓ CUPS

One 14-ounce can reduced-sodium diced tomatoes
One 6-ounce can reduced-sodium tomato paste
2 tablespoons olive oil
4 teaspoons minced oregano leaves or 2 teaspoons dried oregano
2 teaspoons sugar
½ teaspoon salt
8 basil leaves
1 garlic clove, minced

Place the diced tomatoes, tomato paste, olive oil, oregano, sugar, salt, basil leaves, and garlic in a large blender or a food processor. Blend or process until smooth, scraping down the inside of the canister or the bowl as necessary. Store, covered, in a plastic container in the refrigerator for up to 3 days, or freeze any extra in ½-cup plastic containers or zip-closed plastic bags for up to 3 months.

Pizza Pesto

Pesto is a no-cook sauce made from blending together fresh herbs, nuts, and cheese. While basil is the most traditional herb, there's no reason to stand on ceremony, as you can see below. Pesto for a pizza needs to be slightly drier than the kind used on pasta so the sauce doesn't run all over the hot pie on the grill or in the oven. If you use jarred pesto for your pies, pour off the oil that lies on top of the jar, rather than stirring it back into the sauce.

MAKES ABOUT 1½ CUPS

6 tablespoons pine nuts, or chopped walnut pieces, or chopped pecan pieces

3 cups packed basil leaves; or 2 cups packed, stemmed arugula and 1 cup packed basil leaves; or 1½ cups packed sage leaves and 1½ cups packed parsley leaves; or 1 cup packed cilantro leaves, 1 cup packed parsley leaves, and 1 cup packed basil leaves

2½ ounces Parmigiano-Reggiano, finely grated

½ cup olive oil, preferably extra virgin

3 garlic cloves, quartered

½ teaspoon salt

½ teaspoon freshly ground black pepper

1. Place the nuts in a small skillet set over low heat. Cook until aromatic and lightly browned, shaking the pan occasionally so the nuts don't burn, 3 to 5 minutes. Pour into a small bowl and cool for 5 minutes.

2. Place the toasted nuts, herbs, cheese, olive oil, 3 tablespoons water, garlic, salt, and pepper in a food processor. Process until the mixture becomes a grainy paste, scraping down the inside of the bowl as necessary. Since this sauce makes more than you'll need, place the remainder in ½-cup containers, cover with a thin film of olive oil, and freeze for the next time you make a pie; thaw in the refrigerator overnight before using, pouring off the excess olive oil, which has only been used to keep the basil fresh and green. (That flavored oil can now be used for salad dressings and marinades.)

TEN CLASSIC PIES

Pizza Margherita 45

Mushroom Pizza 47

Pepperoni Pizza 50

Four Cheese Pizza 52

Four Seasons Pizza 55

Vegetable Pizza 58

White Clam Pizza 61

Plum Tomato and Fresh Mozzarella Pizza 63

Sausage and Pepper Pizza 66

Spinach and Mushroom Pizza 69

These are the pies we come back to again and again. Sure, it's great to experiment with flavors and tastes, but very little can beat a good pizza Margherita—the classic cheese pie—or a mushroom pizza.

That said, these recipes tweak the standards a bit, more for modern tastes and flavors. We encourage you to use a variety of mushrooms—shiitake, cremini, portobello—for the pies, not just white button mushrooms; we also encourage you to add fresh herbs to the pies, the better to balance the cheese.

Pizza Margherita

There may be no more quintessential pizza: a topping of tomato sauce, mozzarella, and a little seasoning on a perfect crust. The pie is named for Queen Margherita of Italy who made a trip to Naples with her husband, King Umberto I, in 1889. The queen had heard rumors of a dish called "pizza," made at Pietro il Pizzaiolo, a restaurant in town. She asked the owner and his wife, Donna Rosa Esposito, the restaurant's pizza maker, to prepare a few pies in her palazzo. The queen tasted all three but judged this version her favorite—probably because of its fresh taste but also because the tomato sauce, cheese, and basil could be said to represent the three colors of the Italian flag. Politics, like taste, is everything.

MAKES 1 PIZZA

Yellow cornmeal for the pizza peel or nonstick spray for the pizza tray or the baking sheet

One recipe homemade dough, preferably the Classic Pizza Dough (page 23); or 1 pound purchased fresh dough or frozen dough, thawed; or one 12- to 14-inch store-bought, prebaked plain pizza crust

¾ cup Classic Pizza Sauce (page 38), No-Cook Pizza Sauce (page 39), or jarred plain pizza sauce

1 tablespoon minced fresh basil leaves

½ teaspoon freshly ground black pepper, or garlic powder, or onion powder, or red pepper flakes, or mild or hot paprika

8 ounces (½ pound) fresh mozzarella, thinly sliced

BAKING OPTIONS

With a pizza stone. Preheat the stone in the oven at 450°F for 30 to 45 minutes; or preheat the stone on a gas grill at medium, indirect heat (about 450°F) for 30 to 45 minutes; or build an indirect, medium-heat coal bed in a charcoal grill and preheat the stone for the same amount of time.

With a pizza tray or a large baking sheet. Preheat the oven to 450°F, a gas grill to indirect, medium heat (about 450°F), or build an indirect, medium-heat coal bed around the perimeter of a charcoal grill.

CRUST OPTIONS

Fresh dough on a pizza stone. Dust a pizza peel lightly with cornmeal, set the dough at its center, and dimple the dough with your fingertips into a thick, flattened circle. Pick up the dough and shape it with your hands, holding its edge, slowly turning the dough until it's about 14 inches in diameter. Set it floured side down on the peel.

Fresh dough on a pizza tray or a baking sheet. Grease one or the other with non-stick spray. Lay the dough at its center and dimple the dough with your fingertips—then pull and press the dough until it forms a 14-inch circle on the tray or a 12 × 7-inch irregular rectangle on the baking sheet.

A *prebaked crust.* Place it on a pizza peel if you're also using a pizza stone—or place the prebaked crust right on a pizza tray or a large baking sheet.

1. Use a rubber spatula to spread the pizza sauce evenly over the dough, leaving a border of about ½ inch around the edge. Sprinkle with the minced basil and one of the other spices, then lay the mozzarella slices on top.

2. Slide the pie from the peel to the hot stone, or place the pie on its tray or baking sheet in the oven on the middle rack or over the unheated section of the grill. Bake or grill with the lid closed until the cheese has melted and is bubbling and the crust's edge is golden brown, 16 to 18 minutes. If you've used fresh dough, check it a few times during the first 10 minutes to pop any air bubbles that may blow up at its edge or across its surface. Slide the peel back under the hot pie to get it off the stone, then slip the pie off the peel and right onto a wire rack—or transfer the pie on its tray or baking sheet to a wire rack. In any event, cool the pizza for 5 minutes before slicing.

Mushroom Pizza

For this pizza parlor favorite, you can use sliced cremini or white button mushrooms—or make it with all sorts of exotic and wild mushrooms. In the end, they all must be sliced thinly so they cook evenly and quickly. The only other trick? Make sure you sauté them long enough so they give off their liquid in the skillet and it evaporates almost completely—to keep the crust from getting soggy over the heat.

MAKES 1 PIZZA

All-purpose flour for the pizza peel or olive oil for the pizza tray or a large baking sheet

One recipe homemade dough, preferably the Parmesan Pizza Dough (page 31); or 1 pound purchased fresh dough or frozen dough, thawed; or one 12- to 14-inch store-bought, prebaked plain pizza crust

2 tablespoons olive oil

6 garlic cloves, thinly sliced

4 cups cleaned, thinly sliced mushrooms, preferably cremini or white button, or some exotic varietals mixed in with them (see Note)

½ teaspoon red pepper flakes

1 tablespoon Worcestershire sauce

6 tablespoons Classic Pizza Sauce (page 38), or No-Cook Pizza Sauce (page 39), or jarred plain pizza sauce

6 ounces mozzarella, shredded

1 ounce Parmigiano-Reggiano, finely grated

BAKING OPTIONS

With a pizza stone. Preheat the stone in the oven at 450°F for 30 to 45 minutes; or preheat the stone on a gas grill at medium, indirect heat (about 450°F) for 30 to 45 minutes; or build an indirect, medium-heat coal bed in a charcoal grill and preheat the stone for the same amount of time.

With a pizza tray or a large baking sheet. Preheat the oven to 450°F, a gas grill to indirect, medium heat (about 450°F), or build an indirect, medium-heat coal bed around the perimeter of a charcoal grill.

CRUST OPTIONS

Fresh dough on a pizza stone. Dust a pizza peel with flour, set the dough at its center, and form the dough into a large, flat circle by dimpling it with your fingertips. Pick it up by its edge and rotate it, stretching gently, until it's about 14 inches in diameter. Set it floured side down on the peel.

Fresh dough on a pizza tray or a large baking sheet. Grease the tray or baking sheet with olive oil. Lay the dough at the center and dimple the dough with your fingertips—then pull and press it until it forms a 14-inch circle on the tray or an irregular rectangle, about 12 × 7 inches, on the baking sheet.

A prebaked crust. Place it on a floured pizza peel if you're also using a pizza stone—or place the prebaked crust right on a pizza tray or a large baking sheet.

1. Heat the olive oil in a large skillet set over medium heat. Add the garlic and cook for 1 minute, stirring often.

2. Add the mushrooms and red pepper flakes. Cook, stirring often, until the mushrooms give off their liquid. Pour in the Worcestershire sauce; continue cooking, stirring frequently, until any liquid in the pan has been reduced to a glaze, about 5 minutes. Cool at room temperature for 10 minutes.

3. Meanwhile, spread the pizza sauce evenly over the crust, leaving a ½-inch border around the edge. Evenly cover the sauce with the shredded mozzarella.

4. Spoon and spread the mushroom mixture evenly over the cheese, then top with the grated Parmigiano-Reggiano.

5. Slide the pizza from the peel to the preheated stone; if you're using a pizza tray or a baking sheet, place it in the oven or over the unheated section of the grill grate. Bake or grill with the lid closed until the cheese begins to bubble and the crust has firmed up at its edge, 16 to 18 minutes. If you're using fresh pizza dough, check on it a few times during the first 10 minutes so you can pop any air bubbles that may dot its surface or edge. Once the pie is done, slip the peel back under the crust to remove it from the hot stone or use oven mitts to set the tray or baking sheet with its pie on a wire cooling rack. Wait 5 minutes before slicing. If you want to make sure the crust stays crisp, take the pie off the peel, tray, or sheet after a minute or two and let it cool directly on the wire rack.

NOTE: You'll need 12 to 14 ounces of mushrooms to get 4 cups sliced. Avoid portobello caps because they are too big. And use only the caps of shiitake mushrooms, not their fibrous stems. In any case, clean whole mushrooms with damp paper towels.

Pepperoni Pizza

Related to dry salami, pepperoni is an Italian-style sausage, usually made from beef or pork. Of course, you can also use vegetarian pepperoni, made from soy protein but spiced in a similar way. Still, the quality and spiciness of the type you choose will directly affect the pizza's quality. If possible, have it sliced for you at the butcher section of your supermarket.

MAKES 1 PIZZA

All-purpose flour for the pizza peel or olive oil for the pizza tray or the baking sheet

One recipe homemade dough, preferably the Classic Pizza Dough (page 23); or 1 pound purchased fresh dough or frozen dough, thawed; or one 12- to 14-inch store-bought, prebaked plain pizza crust

6 tablespoons Classic Pizza Sauce (page 38), No-Cook Pizza Sauce (page 39), or jarred plain pizza sauce

8 ounces (½ pound) regular, low-fat, fat-free, or soy mozzarella, shredded

3 ounces beef, pork, or soy pepperoni, sliced into thin rings

2 medium shallots, thinly sliced into rings

BAKING OPTIONS

With a pizza stone. Preheat the stone in the oven at 450°F for 30 to 45 minutes; or preheat the stone on a gas grill at medium, indirect heat (about 450°F) for 30 to 45 minutes; or build an indirect, medium-heat fire in a charcoal grill and preheat the stone for the same amount of time.

With a pizza tray or a large baking sheet. Preheat the oven to 450°F, a gas grill to indirect, medium heat (about 450°F), or build an indirect, medium-heat coal bed around the perimeter of a charcoal grill.

CRUST OPTIONS

Fresh dough on a pizza stone. First, dust a pizza peel lightly with flour. Add the dough and form it into a large circle by dimpling it with your fingertips. Pick it up and stretch and rotate it by its edge until it's about 14 inches in diameter. Set it floured side down on the peel.

Fresh dough on a pizza tray or a large baking sheet. Grease either with a little olive oil dabbed on a paper towel. Lay the dough at the center of the pizza tray or baking sheet; dimple the dough with your fingertips—then pull and press it until it forms a 14-inch circle on the tray or an irregular, 12 × 7-inch rectangle on the baking sheet.

A prebaked crust. Place it on a floured pizza peel if you're also using a pizza stone—or place the prebaked crust on a pizza tray or a large baking sheet.

1. Spread the sauce over the prepared crust with a rubber spatula, leaving a ½-inch border at the crust's edge. Top with half the shredded cheese.

2. Lay the pepperoni and shallot slices evenly over the sauce, then top with the other half of the cheese. Taking care not to dislodge the toppings, slide the pizza from the peel to the hot stone; or place the pie on its tray or baking sheet either in the oven or on the part of the grill grate that is not directly over the heat source.

3. Bake or grill with the lid closed until the cheese has melted and the crust is golden and somewhat firm, 16 to 18 minutes. Slide the peel back under the pie to take it off the very hot stone or remove the pie on its tray or baking sheet from the oven or grill and set it on a wire rack. In any event, cool the pizza for 5 minutes before slicing and serving. If you want to make sure the crust stays crisp, transfer the pie from the peel, tray, or baking sheet directly to the wire rack after a minute or two.

Four Cheese Pizza

Although there are many variations of this pizza-parlor favorite, here's our favorite, with a little roasted garlic to help tone down the heaviness of all that cheese. If you'd like to come up with your own combination of four cheeses, keep this in mind: at least two of them should be semifirm cheeses like Cheddar or Monterey Jack; at least one should be a hard cheese like Parmigiano-Reggiano or Grana Padano; and none should be a soft cheese like ricotta or goat cheese. Look for roasted garlic cloves at the salad or deli bar of your local supermarket. Failing that, roast your own, following the instructions in step 1 on page 105.

MAKES 1 PIZZA

Yellow cornmeal for a pizza peel or olive oil for a pizza tray or a large baking
   sheet
One recipe homemade dough, preferably the Classic Pizza Dough (page 23);
   or 1 pound purchased fresh dough or frozen dough, thawed; or one 12- to
   14-inch store-bought, prebaked plain pizza crust
1 head roasted garlic, cloves separated and their husks removed
1 tablespoon olive oil
1 teaspoon Dijon mustard
4 ounces mozzarella, shredded
4 ounces provolone, shredded
4 ounces Muenster, shredded
2 ounces Pecorino, finely grated
½ teaspoon grated nutmeg
½ teaspoon freshly ground black pepper

BAKING OPTIONS

With a pizza stone. Preheat the stone in the oven at 425°F for 30 to 45 minutes; or preheat the stone on a gas grill at medium, indirect heat (about 425°F) for 30

to 45 minutes; or build an indirect, medium-heat fire in a charcoal grill and pre-heat the stone for the same amount of time.

With a pizza tray or a baking sheet. Preheat the oven to 425°F, a gas grill to indirect, medium heat (about 425°F), or build an indirect, medium-heat, well-ashed coal bed around the perimeter of a charcoal grill.

CRUST OPTIONS

Fresh dough on a pizza stone. Dust a pizza peel lightly with cornmeal, then set the dough at its center. Start dimpling the dough, pressing into it with your fingertips as you stretch it slightly, until it's a thick, flattened circle with lots of little ridges. Pick it up by the edge and slowly rotate and stretch the circle until it's about 14 inches in diameter. Set it floured side down on the peel.

Fresh dough on a pizza tray or a large baking sheet. Grease either lightly with some olive oil on a paper towel. Lay the dough on the tray or baking sheet and dimple the dough with your fingertips until it's a flattened circle—then pull and press it until it forms a 14-inch circle on the pizza tray or an irregular rectangle, about 12 inches long by 7 inches wide, on the baking sheet.

A prebaked crust. Place it on a pizza peel if you're also using a pizza stone—or place the prebaked crust right on a pizza tray or a large baking sheet.

1. Puree the roasted garlic cloves, olive oil, and Dijon mustard in a mini food processor until a smooth paste is formed or mash these three together in a small bowl with a fork until pastelike and fairly smooth. Spread this mixture evenly over the crust, leaving a ½-inch border at its edge.

2. Mix the four kinds of cheese in a large bowl, then sprinkle evenly over the roasted garlic paste on the crust. Sprinkle the nutmeg and pepper over the pizza.

3. Slip the pizza from the peel to the heated stone or place the pie on its tray or baking sheet either in the oven or on the grill over indirect heat. Bake or grill with the lid closed until the cheese has melted and just started to turn brown in patches, 16 to 18 minutes. Slip the peel back under the pie to take it off the stone and cool for 5 minutes before slicing—or transfer the pie on its tray or baking sheet to a wire rack to cool slightly before slicing. To ensure the crust stays crisp, you can also transfer the pie from the peel, tray, or baking sheet right to the wire rack after a minute or so, then continue cooling as directed.

Four Seasons Pizza

or this traditional pie (known as a *quattro stagione* in Italian), the crust is divided into four equal quadrants, each representing one of the seasons: mushrooms for the fall, prosciutto for the winter, artichoke hearts for the spring, and olives for the summer. But you can just as easily mix all these ingredients together over the top of the pie so everyone gets a little of every season.

MAKES 1 PIZZA

All-purpose flour for the pizza peel or olive oil for the pizza tray or the baking sheet

One recipe homemade dough, preferably the Parmesan Pizza Dough (page 31); or 1 pound purchased fresh dough or frozen dough, thawed; or one 12- to 14-inch store-bought, prebaked plain pizza crust

½ cup Classic Pizza Sauce (page 38), No-Cook Pizza Sauce (page 39), or jarred plain pizza sauce

6 ounces fresh mozzarella, thinly sliced

3 ounces thinly sliced prosciutto

1 cup sliced shiitake mushroom caps or sliced cremini mushrooms (about 3 ounces)

1 cup frozen quartered artichoke hearts, thawed and squeezed dry of their excess moisture

½ cup sliced pitted green or black olives

2 ounces Parmigiano-Reggiano, grated

BAKING OPTIONS

With a pizza stone. Position the rack in the middle of the oven and preheat the stone in the oven at 450°F for 30 to 45 minutes; or preheat the stone on a gas grill at medium, indirect heat (about 450°F) for 30 to 45 minutes; or build an indirect, medium-heat coal bed in a charcoal grill and then preheat the stone for the same amount of time.

With a pizza tray or a large baking sheet. Preheat the oven to 450°F, a gas grill to indirect, medium heat (about 450°F), or build an indirect, medium-heat fire around the perimeter of a charcoal grill.

CRUST OPTIONS

Fresh dough on a pizza stone. Dust a pizza peel with flour, then set the dough at its center. Dimple the dough with your fingertips until it's a thick, flattened circle. Pick it up and shape it into a circle about 14 inches in diameter by stretching and rotating it while holding its edge. Set it floured side down on the peel.

Fresh dough on a pizza tray or a large baking sheet. Grease one or the other with some olive oil dabbed on a paper towel. Lay the dough on the tray or baking sheet, then dimple the dough until it's a thick, flattened circle. Pull and press the dough until it forms a 14-inch circle on the tray or an irregular 12 × 7-inch rectangle on the baking sheet.

A prebaked crust. Place it on a pizza peel if you're also using a pizza stone—or place the prebaked crust on a pizza tray or a large baking sheet.

1. Spread the pizza sauce evenly over the dough, leaving a ½-inch border at the edge. Lay the mozzarella slices evenly over the sauce.

2. Imagining the dough in four equal quarters, lay the prosciutto, mushrooms, artichoke hearts, and olives in each of those quarters. Sprinkle the grated Parmigiano-Reggiano over the whole pie.

3. Slip the pie from the peel onto the stone or place the pie on its tray or baking sheet in the oven or onto the unheated portion of the grill. Bake or grill with the lid closed until the cheese has melted and the crust is a golden brown, 16 to 18 minutes. If you're working with fresh dough, check it occasionally to make sure no air pockets or bubbles have arisen on its surface; flatten or pop any that do.

4. Slip the peel back under the crust to remove the pie from the stone and set aside to cool for 5 minutes—or transfer the pie on its tray or baking sheet to a wire rack to cool for 5 minutes. Before serving, slice the pizza into at least 8 wedges, respecting the various divisions of the ingredients.

Vegetable Pizza

If you want to turn this pie into a vegan entrée, use soy mozzarella for both cheeses. But no matter how you make it, this is a simple pizza, a standard in the repertory, best as lunch or dinner off the grill on a summer Saturday.

MAKES 1 PIZZA

Yellow cornmeal to dust the pizza peel or olive oil to grease the pizza tray or the baking sheet

One recipe homemade dough, preferably the Semolina Pizza Dough (page 29) or the Cracker Pizza Dough (page 35); or 1 pound purchased fresh dough or frozen dough, thawed; or one 12- to 14-inch store-bought, prebaked plain pizza crust

½ cup Classic Pizza Sauce (page 38), No-Cook Pizza Sauce (page 39), or jarred plain pizza sauce

6 ounces soft goat cheese, such as Montrachet

2½ cups frozen mixed vegetables, thawed; or mixed, prepared, quick-cooking fresh vegetables, such as seeded and diced bell pepper, diced zucchini or summer squash, thinly sliced red onion, frozen peas, broccoli florets, cauliflower florets, and/or roasted garlic cloves (see page 105)

¼ cup shredded basil leaves (do not use dried basil)

2 ounces Parmigiano-Reggiano, finely grated

½ teaspoon freshly ground black pepper or red pepper flakes, optional

BAKING OPTIONS

With a pizza tray or a large baking sheet. Preheat the oven to 450°F, a gas grill to indirect, medium heat (about 450°F), or build an indirect, medium-heat fire around the perimeter of a charcoal grill.

With a pizza stone. Preheat the stone in the oven at 450°F for 30 to 45 minutes; or preheat the stone on a gas grill at medium, indirect heat (about 450°F) for

30 to 45 minutes; or build an indirect, medium-heat coal bed in a charcoal grill and preheat the stone for the same amount of time.

CRUST OPTIONS

Fresh dough on a pizza stone. First, dust a pizza peel lightly with cornmeal. Add the dough and form it into a large circle by dimpling it with your fingertips. Pick it up and shape it with your hands holding its edge, slowly turning the circle and stretching the edge until it's about 14 inches in diameter. The Cracker Pizza Dough is too fragile to pick up like this; see page 35 for an explanation of the special technique it requires. In any event, set the dough cornmeal side down on the peel.

Fresh dough on a pizza tray or a large baking sheet. Grease the tray or baking sheet with some olive oil dabbed on a paper towel. Lay the dough on either and form the dough into a thick, flat circle by dimpling it with your fingertips—then pull and press it until it forms a 14-inch circle on the tray or an irregular rectangle, about 12×7 inches, on the baking sheet.

A prebaked crust. Place it on a cornmeal-dusted pizza peel if you're also using a pizza stone—or place the prebaked crust on a pizza tray or a large baking sheet.

1. Spread the pizza sauce over the pressed-out crust, taking care to leave a ½--inch border at its edge. Crumble the goat cheese evenly over the sauce.

2. Top with the vegetables, arranging them in a decorative pattern over the pie.

3. Sprinkle with the shredded basil and then the grated Parmigiano-Reggiano. Finally, sprinkle with the pepper or red pepper flakes, if desired.

4. Slide the pie from the peel to the hot stone or set the pie on its tray or baking sheet either in the oven or over the unheated portion of the grill. Bake or grill with the lid closed until the cheese is bubbling and the crust is golden brown at its edge, taking care to pop any air bubbles that may arise across fresh dough, about 17 minutes. Slide the peel back under the very hot pie and set it aside to cool for 5 minutes before slicing—or transfer the pie on its tray or baking sheet to a wire rack to cool for 5 minutes before slicing. To ensure the crust stays crisp, consider transferring the hot pie directly to the wire rack after a couple of minutes.

White Clam Pizza

Although many people make their "white" pizzas with canned clams, look for frozen, chopped clams in the frozen seafood case of many supermarkets. These will give you a brighter, brinier taste, less tinned and certainly more sophisticated. Do not use dried parsley; only fresh can stand up to the clams.

MAKES 1 PIZZA

Either all-purpose flour for the pizza peel or olive oil for the pizza tray or a large baking sheet

One recipe homemade dough, preferably the Semolina Pizza Dough (page 29) or the Parmesan Pizza Dough (page 31); or 1 pound purchased fresh dough or frozen dough, thawed; or one 12- to 14-inch store-bought, prebaked plain pizza crust

2 tablespoons olive oil

6 garlic cloves, minced

½ teaspoon red pepper flakes

12 ounces (¾ pound) frozen chopped clams, thawed; or two 6- or 7-ounce cans clams, drained

2 tablespoons dry white wine or dry vermouth

2 tablespoons chopped parsley leaves

1½ ounces Pecorino, finely grated

BAKING OPTIONS

With a pizza stone. Preheat the stone in the oven at 450°F for 30 to 45 minutes; or preheat the stone on a gas grill at medium, indirect heat (about 450°F) for 30 to 45 minutes; or build an indirect, medium-heat fire in a charcoal grill and preheat the stone for the same amount of time.

With a pizza tray or a large baking sheet. Preheat the oven to 450°F, a gas grill to indirect, medium heat (about 450°F), or build an indirect, medium-heat coal bed around the perimeter of a charcoal grill.

CRUST OPTIONS

Fresh dough on a pizza stone. Dust a pizza peel with flour, set the dough at its center, and form the dough into a large, thick circle by dimpling it with your fingertips. Pick it up with its edge in both hands and slowly rotate it, stretching it all the while, until the circle is about 14 inches in diameter. Set the dough floured side down on the peel.

Fresh dough on a pizza tray or a large baking sheet. Grease one or the other with some olive oil dabbed on a paper towel. Lay the dough at the center of either; dimple the dough into a thick, flat circle with your fingertips—then pull and press it until it forms a 14-inch circle on the tray or a 12 × 7-inch somewhat irregular rectangle on the baking sheet.

A prebaked crust. Place it on a floured pizza peel if you're also using a pizza stone—or place the prebaked crust on a pizza tray or a large baking sheet.

1. Heat a large skillet over medium heat. Swirl in the olive oil, then add the garlic and red pepper flakes. Cook, stirring constantly, for 30 seconds.

2. Stir in the clams, wine, and the parsley; bring to a simmer and cook, stirring often, until the liquid has reduced to a glaze, about 2 minutes.

3. Spread the clam mixture evenly over the prepared crust, leaving a ½-inch border. Top with the grated Pecorino.

4. Slide the pie from the peel to the hot stone or place the pie on its tray or baking sheet either in the oven or over the part of the grill grate that's not directly over the heat or the coals. Bake or grill with the lid closed until the crust is somewhat firm and lightly browned, 14 to 16 minutes. Slip the peel back under the pie to get the pizza off the hot stone or transfer the pie on its tray or baking sheet to a wire rack. Set aside to cool for 5 minutes before slicing.

Plum Tomato and Fresh Mozzarella Pizza

Rather than using tomato sauce as with a Pizza Margherita (page 45), this pie calls for fresh tomatoes. Oblong plum tomatoes, also known as Roma tomatoes, are the best bet when summer's far away. They're sweeter and more flavorful than those big, red spheres of fibrous, shaped water that appear in markets all winter long. If it's summer and tomatoes are on the vine, feel free to substitute whatever's fresh.

MAKES 1 PIZZA

All-purpose flour for dusting the pizza peel or olive oil for greasing the pizza tray or the baking sheet

One recipe homemade dough, preferably the Olive Oil Pizza Dough (page 27); or 1 pound purchased fresh dough or frozen dough, thawed; or one 12- to 14-inch store-bought, prebaked plain pizza crust

8 ounces (½ pound) fresh mozzarella, thinly sliced

8 to 12 large basil leaves

3 medium plum or Roma tomatoes, thinly sliced

4 garlic cloves, minced

2 teaspoons minced oregano leaves, or parsley leaves, or marjoram leaves, or stemmed thyme leaves

½ teaspoon salt, preferably coarse kosher salt

½ teaspoon freshly ground black pepper

1 tablespoon extra virgin olive oil

BAKING OPTIONS

With a pizza stone. Position the rack in the middle of the oven and preheat the stone in the oven at 450°F for 30 to 45 minutes; or preheat the stone on a gas grill at medium, indirect heat (about 450°F) for 30 to 45 minutes; or build an

indirect, medium-heat coal bed in a charcoal grill and then preheat the stone for the same amount of time.

With a pizza tray or a large baking sheet. Preheat the oven to 450°F, a gas grill to indirect, medium heat (about 450°F), or build an indirect, medium-heat fire around the perimeter of a charcoal grill.

CRUST OPTIONS

Fresh dough on a pizza stone. Dust a pizza peel with flour, set the dough at its center, and form the dough into a large circle by dimpling it with your fingertips. Pick it up and shape it by holding its edge as you gently rotate and stretch the dough until it's about 14 inches in diameter. Set it floured side down on the peel.

Fresh dough on a pizza tray or a large baking sheet. Grease one or the other with some olive oil dabbed on a paper towel. Lay the dough on either and dimple the dough with your fingertips—then pull and press the dough until it forms a 14-inch circle on the tray or a 12 × 7-inch irregular rectangle on the baking sheet.

A prebaked crust. Place it on a floured pizza peel if you're also using a pizza stone—or place the prebaked crust right on a pizza tray or a large baking sheet.

1. Lay the sliced mozzarella evenly over the dough or crust, leaving a ½-inch border around its edge; then tuck in the basil leaves among the slices.

2. Place the tomatoes on top, then sprinkle the minced garlic, herb, salt, and pepper evenly over the tomatoes and cheese.

3. Slip the crust off the peel and onto the stone or place the pie on its tray or baking sheet in the oven or on the grill; bake or grill with the lid closed until the cheese has melted and is bubbling and the crust is firm and lightly browned,

16 to 18 minutes. If you've used fresh dough, check the pizza after about 10 minutes to pop any air bubbles that may form around the crust's rim.

4. Slip the peel back under the crust to remove from the stone or transfer the pie on its tray or baking sheet to a wire rack. Drizzle the extra virgin olive oil over the pizza, then cool for 5 minutes before slicing. If you want to keep the crust fairly crunchy, consider transferring the pie from the peel, tray, or baking sheet right onto the wire rack after a couple of minutes.

Sausage and Pepper Pizza

Although we call for sweet Italian sausage, the favorite for this pie, you can certainly substitute any kind of pork or beef sausage—or a combination of both hot and sweet Italian sausage. But since you need to use loose sausage meat, not in casings, chicken and turkey sausages are not the best bet.

MAKES 1 PIZZA

All-purpose flour for dusting the pizza peel or olive oil for greasing the pizza tray or the baking sheet

One recipe homemade dough, preferably the Classic Pizza Dough (page 23); or 1 pound purchased fresh dough or frozen dough, thawed; or one 12- to 14-inch store-bought, prebaked plain pizza crust

12 ounces (¾ pound) sweet Italian sausage, casings removed

2 teaspoons olive oil

3 tablespoons Classic Pizza Sauce (page 38), No-Cook Pizza Sauce (page 39), or jarred plain pizza sauce

6 ounces mozzarella, shredded

1 medium green bell pepper, seeded and diced

1 medium jarred roasted red pepper or pimiento, diced

1 ounce Parmigiano-Reggiano, finely grated

BAKING OPTIONS

With a pizza tray or a large baking sheet. Preheat the oven to 450°F, a gas grill to indirect, medium heat (about 450°F), or build an indirect, medium-heat coal bed around the perimeter of a charcoal grill.

With a pizza stone. Preheat the stone in the oven at 450°F for 30 to 45 minutes; or preheat the stone on a gas grill at medium, indirect heat (about 450°F) for 30 to 45 minutes; or build an indirect, medium-heat coal bed in a charcoal grill and preheat the stone for the same amount of time.

CRUST OPTIONS

Fresh dough on a pizza stone. First, dust a pizza peel with flour. Add the dough and form it into a large circle by dimpling it with your fingertips. Pick it up and shape it with your hands, holding its edge, slowly turning the dough until it's about 14 inches in diameter. Set the shaped dough floured side down on the peel.

Fresh dough on a pizza tray or a large baking sheet. Grease the tray or baking sheet with some olive oil dabbed onto a paper towel. Lay the dough on either and dimple the dough with your fingertips until it's a thick, flat circle—then pull and press it until it forms a 14-inch circle on the tray or a 12 × 7-inch irregular rectangle on the baking sheet.

A prebaked crust. Place it on a floured pizza peel if you're also using a pizza stone—or place the prebaked crust on a pizza tray or a large baking sheet.

1. Sauté the sausage with the olive oil in a medium skillet set over medium heat until browned and cooked through, stirring often, about 4 minutes. Drain the excess fat and liquid in the skillet.

2. Spread the pizza sauce evenly over the prepared crust, leaving a ½-inch border at its edge. Top with the shredded mozzarella, then with the cooked sausage.

3. Sprinkle both the diced bell pepper and jarred red pepper or pimiento over the pie, then top with the grated Parmigiano-Reggiano.

4. Slide the pizza from the peel to the hot stone, taking care not to lose the toppings along the way—or place the pie on its tray or baking sheet with its pizza either in the oven or on the unheated part of the grill grate, the part that's not directly over the heat.

5. Bake or grill with the lid closed until the cheese has melted and the crust is firm, 16 to 18 minutes. If any air bubbles arise across the fresh dough, prick them with a fork. Slip the peel back under the pie to remove it from the hot stone—or place the pie on its tray or baking sheet with its pizza on a wire rack. Set aside to cool for 5 minutes before slicing. To make sure the crust stays crisp, consider transferring the pie from the peel, tray, or baking sheet right to the wire rack after a minute or so.

Spinach and Mushroom Pizza

For this Italian-American classic, use only baby spinach leaves, some-times sold in boxes in the salad section of the supermarket's produce case. They're more tender and lack the astringent bite of their larger, leafier kin.

MAKES 1 PIZZA

All-purpose flour for the pizza peel or olive oil for the pizza tray or the baking sheet

One recipe homemade dough, preferably the Parmesan Pizza Dough (page 31); or 1 pound purchased fresh dough or frozen dough, thawed; or one 12- to 14-inch store-bought, prebaked plain pizza crust

2 tablespoons olive oil

12 ounces (¾ pound) cremini mushrooms, cleaned and chopped

10 ounces baby spinach leaves

1 garlic clove, minced

2 tablespoons sweet vermouth or port

2 teaspoons stemmed thyme leaves or 1 teaspoon dried thyme

½ teaspoon salt

½ teaspoon freshly ground black pepper

¼ teaspoon grated or ground nutmeg

4 ounces Gruyère or Emmental, shredded

1½ ounces Parmigiano-Reggiano, finely grated

BAKING OPTIONS

With a pizza stone. Preheat the stone in the oven at 450°F for 30 to 45 minutes; or preheat the stone on a gas grill at medium, indirect heat (about 450°F) for 30 to 45 minutes; or build an indirect, medium-heat coal bed in a charcoal grill and preheat the stone for the same amount of time.

With a pizza tray or a large baking sheet. Preheat the oven to 450°F, a gas grill to indirect, medium heat (about 450°F), or build an indirect, medium-heat fire around the perimeter of a charcoal grill.

CRUST OPTIONS

Fresh dough on a pizza stone. First, dust a pizza peel lightly with flour. Add the dough and form it into a large circle by dimpling it with your fingertips. Pick it up and shape it with your hands holding its edge, slowly turning the dough until it's about 14 inches in diameter. Set the dough floured side down on the peel.

Fresh dough on a pizza tray or a large baking sheet. Grease either one with a little olive oil on a piece of paper towel. Lay the dough on either; dimple the dough with your fingertips until it's a thick, flat circle—then pull and press it until it forms a 14-inch circle on the tray or an irregular 12 × 7-inch rectangle on the baking sheet.

A prebaked *crust.* Place it on a floured pizza peel if you're also using a pizza stone—or place the prebaked crust on a pizza tray or a large baking sheet.

1. Heat a large skillet over medium heat. Swirl in the olive oil, then add the mushrooms. Cook, stirring occasionally, until they give off their liquid and it reduces to a glaze, about 5 minutes.

2. Add the spinach and garlic; toss until the spinach has wilted. Then pour in the sweet vermouth or port, thyme, salt, pepper, and nutmeg. Continue cooking, stirring constantly, until the skillet is dry. Immediately remove the skillet from the heat and set aside.

3. Top the prepared crust with the shredded Gruyère, leaving a ½-inch border at its edge. Spoon and spread the spinach mixture evenly over the cheese.

4. Top with the grated Parmigiano-Reggiano. Slide the pie from the peel onto the hot stone or place the pie on its tray or baking sheet with the pie either in the oven or on the section of the grill grate that's not directly over the gas jets or the coals.

5. Bake or grill with the lid closed until the crust is golden at its edge and the cheese has melted, 16 to 18 minutes. If you're working with fresh dough, check it occasionally so you can prick any air bubbles that may arise on its surface. Once the pie's done, slip the peel back under it to take it off the stone or transfer the pie on its tray or baking sheet to a wire rack. Cool for 5 minutes before slicing. To ensure the crust stays crisp, transfer the pie from the peel, tray, or baking sheet directly to the wire rack after a minute or so.

FOURTEEN
APPETIZER PIZZAS

Antipasto Pizza 77

Artichoke, Olive, and Feta Pizza 80

Winter Squash, Onion, and Pine Nut Pizza 83

Zucchini, Lemon, and Almond Pizza 86

Cherry Tomato and Pancetta Pizza 89

Portobello and Sun-Dried Tomato Pizza 92

Pesto and Dried Cranberry Pizza 94

Fig and Prosciutto Pizza 96

Smoked Salmon Pizza 99

Tuna and White Bean Pizza 102

Corn Relish and Roasted Garlic Pizza 104

Watermelon Pizza 107

Focaccia, Pizza Style 110

Pissaladière, Pizza Style 112

Some pies don't quite make a full meal. Oh, sure, you could round them out with a tossed salad on the side. But these pizzas are probably best with beer, wine, cocktails, or iced tea before dinner. They're light and flavorful, a few simple ingredients making a big splash with the cheese and dough. Have one at the ready when friends drop by. They'll be even better friends within minutes.

Antipasto Pizza

The antipasto platter is often our favorite part of an Italian meal: all the peppers, sun-dried tomatoes, cheeses, and other goodies, often served with crunchy bread. So we've spread those favorites on a pizza crust, a perfect match with a bottle of floral, Italian white wine. If you don't want to buy whole jars of all these items, look for marinated artichoke hearts, green Italian pepperoncini, and pitted black olives on the salad bar at your supermarket.

MAKES 1 PIZZA

Yellow cornmeal for dusting the pizza peel or olive oil for greasing the pizza tray or the baking sheet

One recipe homemade dough, preferably the Semolina Pizza Dough (page 29) or the Cracker Pizza Dough (page 35); or 1 pound purchased fresh dough or frozen dough, thawed; or one 12- to 14-inch store-bought, prebaked plain pizza crust

3 ounces sun-dried tomatoes packed in oil (about 16 sun-dried tomatoes)

3 ounces provolone, cut into very thin slices

6 ounces marinated artichoke hearts, drained and chopped

2 tablespoons chopped, stemmed pepperoncini (about 3 large)

2 tablespoons chopped pitted black olives

1 ounce Parmigiano-Reggiano, finely grated

BAKING OPTIONS

With a pizza stone. Preheat the stone in the oven at 450°F for 30 to 45 minutes; or preheat the stone on a gas grill at medium, indirect heat (about 450°F) for 30 to 45 minutes; or build an indirect, medium-heat fire in a charcoal grill and preheat the stone for the same amount of time.

With a pizza tray or a baking sheet. Preheat the oven to 450°F, a gas grill to indirect, medium heat (about 450°F), or build an indirect, medium-heat coal bed around the perimeter of a charcoal grill.

CRUST OPTIONS

Fresh dough on a pizza stone. First, lightly dust a pizza peel with cornmeal. Place the dough in a mound in the center of the peel and form that dough into a large circle by dimpling it with your fingertips. Then pick it up and shape it with your hands into a circle about 14 inches in diameter. Set it cornmeal side down onto the peel. Note: this forming and shaping technique will not work with the Cracker Pizza Dough—see page 35 for those instructions.

Fresh dough on a pizza tray or a baking sheet. Lightly grease a pizza tray or a large baking sheet with olive oil. Lay the dough on the tray or baking sheet; dimple it with your fingertips—then pull and press the dough until it forms a 14-inch circle on the tray or an irregular rectangle, about 13 inches long and about 7 inches wide, on the baking sheet.

A prebaked crust. Place it on a pizza peel if you're also using a pizza stone—or place the prebaked crust right on a pizza tray or large baking sheet.

1. Process the sun-dried tomatoes in a mini food processor or a food processor fitted with the chopping blade until smooth. Alternatively, mince the sun-dried tomatoes with a chef's knife by rocking the knife repeatedly through them on a cutting board—then take these minced bits and grind them in a mortar with a pestle until smooth.

2. Spread the sun-dried tomato puree over the crust, leaving a ½-inch border at its edge. Lay the provolone slices over the sauce.

3. Sprinkle the artichoke hearts, pepperoncini, and black olives over the pizza; then top with the grated Parmigiano-Reggiano. Slide the pizza from the peel to the hot stone or place the pizza on its tray or baking sheet either in the oven or on the section of the grill grate that's not directly over the heat source.

4. Bake or grill with the lid closed until the crust has turned golden brown and the cheese has melted, 16 to 18 minutes. If you're working with fresh dough, you'll need to check it occasionally so you can pop any air bubbles that may arise at its edges or across its surface. Slip the peel back under the crust to remove it from the very hot stone (be careful not to dislodge the toppings)—or transfer the pizza on its tray or baking sheet to a wire rack. In either case, set aside to cool for 5 minutes before slicing. If desired, remove the pizza from the peel, tray, or baking sheet after a couple of minutes and transfer it directly to the wire rack to cool some more, thereby ensuring that the crust stays crispy. However, if you've used the cracker crust, it may well be too delicate to disturb and is thus better off left on the peel, tray, or baking sheet to avoid a broken pie.

Artichoke, Olive, and Feta Pizza

Use only fresh herbs for this Greek-inspired pizza; they'll better complement the creamy feta. For the best taste, search out grainy sheep's or goat's milk feta, stored in brine at the cheese counter of most supermarkets.

MAKES 1 PIZZA

All-purpose flour for the pizza peel or olive oil for the pizza tray or the large baking sheet

One recipe homemade dough, preferably the Classic Pizza Dough (page 23) or the Olive Oil Pizza Dough (page 27); or 1 pound purchased fresh dough or frozen dough, thawed; or one 12- to 14-inch store-bought, prebaked plain pizza crust

½ cup pitted green or black olives (see Note)

One 10-ounce package frozen quartered artichoke hearts, thawed

3 tablespoons chopped dill, or oregano leaves, or a combination of the two

2 ounces feta

1 medium lemon, quartered

BAKING OPTIONS

With a pizza stone. Position the rack in the middle of the oven and preheat the stone in the oven at 450°F for 30 to 45 minutes; or preheat the stone on a gas grill at medium, indirect heat (about 450°F) for 30 to 45 minutes; or build an indirect, medium-heat coal bed in a charcoal grill and then preheat the stone for the same amount of time.

With a baking sheet. Preheat the oven to 450°F, a gas grill to indirect, medium heat (about 450°F), or build an indirect, medium-heat coal bed around the perimeter of a charcoal grill.

CRUST OPTIONS

Fresh dough on a pizza stone. First, lightly dust a pizza peel with flour. Set the dough in the middle of the peel, then dimple the dough with your fingertips into a large circle. Pick it up and shape it until it's about 14 inches in diameter. Set it floured side down on the peel.

Fresh dough baked on a pizza tray or a baking sheet. Use a little olive oil dabbed on a paper towel to grease a pizza tray or a large baking sheet. Lay the dough on the tray or baking sheet, then dimple it with your fingertips until it's a flattened circle. Pull and press the dough until it forms a 14-inch circle on the tray or an irregular rectangle, about 13 inches long and 7 inches wide, on the baking sheet.

A prebaked crust. Place it on a pizza peel if you're also using a pizza stone—or place the prebaked crust right on a pizza tray or a large baking sheet.

1. Mince the olives on a cutting board with a large knife, rocking it repeatedly through them and gathering them together often, until they're a grainy paste. Alternatively, place them in a mini food processor and process until they have that same grainy consistency.

2. Squeeze the thawed artichoke hearts in batches over the sink, removing as much excess moisture as possible without shredding the hearts themselves. Toss these with the dill in a medium bowl.

3. Spread the olive paste over the crust, leaving a ¼-inch border all around the edge. Top with the herbed artichoke hearts, then finely crumble the feta over the pizza, again keeping that border intact at the crust's edge.

4. Slip the crust off the peel and onto the stone or place the tray or baking sheet in the oven or on the grill. Bake or grill with the lid closed until the cheese has melted and is bubbling and the crust is firm and lightly browned, 14 to 16 minutes.

If using fresh dough, check the pizza after about 10 minutes to pop any air bubbles that may form around the crust's rim. Slip the peel back under the crust to remove from the stone—or transfer the pizza tray or the baking sheet with its pie to a wire rack. To ensure that the crust stays crispy, consider removing the still-hot pie from the peel, tray, or baking sheet and setting it directly on the wire rack. Cool for 5 minutes, then squeeze the lemon juice over the pie before slicing.

NOTE: If desired, skip mincing or processing the olives and simply use ¼ cup purchased green or black olive tapenade.

Winter Squash, Onion, and Pine Nut Pizza

This flavorful, autumnal pie uses winter squash puree as the pizza topping; the puree is then spread like a sauce on the crust. You can find pureed winter squash (sometimes labeled "pureed acorn squash" or "pureed butternut squash") in the freezer section of most supermarkets. Thaw according to the package instructions before using.

MAKES 1 PIZZA

Yellow cornmeal to dust the pizza peel or nonstick spray to grease the pizza tray or the baking sheet

One recipe homemade dough, preferably the Semolina Pizza Dough (page 29); or 1 pound purchased fresh dough or frozen dough, thawed; or one 12- to 14-inch store-bought, prebaked plain pizza crust

2 tablespoons olive oil

2 medium yellow onions, halved through the stem, then thinly sliced

¾ cup frozen winter squash puree, thawed

2 teaspoons minced sage leaves or 1 teaspoon rubbed sage

¼ teaspoon grated or ground nutmeg

¼ teaspoon salt

¼ teaspoon freshly ground black pepper

1½ ounces Parmigiano-Reggiano, or Grana Padano, or Pecorino, finely grated

1 tablespoon pine nuts

BAKING OPTIONS

With a pizza stone. Preheat the stone in the oven at 450°F for 30 to 45 minutes; or preheat the stone on a gas grill at medium, indirect heat (about 450°F) for 30 to 45 minutes; or build an indirect, medium-heat coal bed in a charcoal grill and preheat the stone for the same amount of time.

With a pizza tray or a large baking sheet. Preheat the oven to 450°F, a gas grill to indirect, medium heat (about 450°F), or build an indirect, medium-heat fire around the perimeter of a charcoal grill.

CRUST OPTIONS

Fresh dough on a pizza stone. First, dust a pizza peel lightly with cornmeal. Add the dough and form it into a large circle by dimpling it with your fingertips. Pick it up and shape it by slowly turning it by its edge, stretching that edge all the while, until the circle is about 14 inches in diameter. Set it cornmeal side down on the peel.

Fresh dough on a pizza tray or a large baking sheet. Grease the tray or baking sheet lightly with nonstick spray. Lay the dough on the tray or baking sheet and dimple it with your fingertips—then pull and press it until it forms a circle about 14 inches in diameter on the pizza tray or a 12 × 7-inch somewhat irregular rectangle on the baking sheet.

A prebaked crust. Place it on a cornmeal-dusted pizza peel if you're also using a pizza stone—or place the prebaked crust on a pizza tray or a large baking sheet.

1. Heat a large skillet over medium heat, then swirl in the olive oil. Add the onion slices, reduce the heat to very low, and cook, stirring often, until soft, golden, and very sweet, 20 to 25 minutes.

2. Meanwhile, stir the squash puree, sage, nutmeg, salt, and pepper in a medium bowl until uniform. Spread this mixture evenly over the prepared crust, leaving a ½-inch border at its edge.

3. Top with the caramelized onions, then sprinkle the grated Parmigiano-Reggiano and pine nuts over the pie. Slide the pizza from the peel to the very hot stone or place the pie on its tray or baking sheet either in the oven or on the section of the grill grate that's not right over the heat source.

4. Bake or grill with the lid closed until the crust is golden and somewhat firm to the touch, perhaps even a little darkened on its bottom, 16 to 18 minutes. If using fresh dough, prick any air bubbles that may arise so the crust will be even. Slip the peel back under the pie to get it off the stone or set the pie on its tray or the baking sheet on a wire rack. Cool for 5 minutes before slicing. If you want to make sure the crust stays crunchy, consider transferring the pie directly to the wire rack after a minute or so.

Zucchini, Lemon, and Almond Pizza

We first tasted an appetizer of zucchini, lemons, and almonds at the Red Cat restaurant in New York City years ago—and we've been hooked on the combination ever since.

MAKES 1 PIZZA

Either yellow cornmeal for the pizza peel or nonstick spray for the pizza tray or the baking sheet

One recipe homemade dough, preferably the Semolina Pizza Dough (page 29); or 1 pound purchased fresh dough or frozen dough, thawed; or one 12- to 14-inch store-bought, prebaked plain pizza crust

1 large green zucchini, shredded through the large holes of a box grater or with the shredding blade in a food processor

1 teaspoon salt

1 large lemon

2 ounces Parmigiano-Reggiano, finely grated

2 tablespoons sliced almonds

BAKING OPTIONS

With a pizza stone. Preheat the stone in the oven at 450°F for 30 to 45 minutes; or preheat the stone on a gas grill at medium, indirect heat (about 450°F) for 30 to 45 minutes; or build an indirect, medium-heat coal bed in a charcoal grill and preheat the stone for the same amount of time.

With a pizza tray or a large baking sheet. Preheat the oven to 450°F, a gas grill to indirect, medium heat (about 450°F), or build an indirect, medium-heat coal bed around the perimeter of a charcoal grill.

CRUST OPTIONS

Fresh dough on a pizza stone. Dust a pizza peel with cornmeal, set the dough at its center, and form the dough into a large, flat circle by dimpling it with your fingertips. Pick the dough up and hold its edge with both hands; slowly rotate the dough, gently stretching its edge all the while, until the circle is about 14 inches in diameter. Set it cornmeal side down on the peel.

Fresh dough on a pizza tray or a large baking sheet. Grease the tray or baking sheet with nonstick spray; set the dough at the center of either. Form the dough into a flat, thick circle by dimpling it with your fingertips—then pull and press it until it forms a 14-inch circle on the tray or an irregular rectangle, about 12×7 inches, on the baking sheet.

A prebaked crust. Place it on a cornmeal-dusted pizza peel if you're also using a pizza stone—or place the prebaked crust on a pizza tray or a large baking sheet.

1. Toss the zucchini with the salt in a large colander, then set in the sink to drain for 30 minutes, tossing occasionally.

2. Meanwhile, place the lemon in a large saucepan, cover with water to a depth of a couple of inches over the lemon, and bring to a boil over high heat. Cover, reduce the heat to medium, and boil until the skin is very soft, about 25 minutes. Drain in a second colander set in the sink and cool at room temperature for 10 minutes.

3. Working in batches, squeeze the zucchini shreds over the sink to remove as much liquid as possible. Place in a large bowl.

4. Cut the lemon in half, then use a spoon to scoop out and discard the hot pulp. Shred the rind through the large holes of a box grater and add it to the zucchini shreds. Toss until well combined, then spread this mixture evenly over the prepared crust, leaving a ½-inch border at its edge.

5. Top with the grated Parmigiano-Reggiano and then the sliced almonds. Slip the pie from the peel to the hot stone or place the pie on its tray or baking sheet either in the oven or on the part of the grill grate that's not right over the heat source.

6. Bake or grill with the lid closed until the crust is golden brown at its edge and somewhat firm, 16 to 18 minutes. If using fresh dough of any kind, check it occasionally so you can prick any air bubbles that might form, particularly at its edge. Slip the peel back under the pie to take it off the stone or remove the pie on its tray or baking sheet from the oven or the grill and place on a wire rack. Cool for 5 minutes before slicing. If you'd like to keep the crust crisp, consider transferring the hot pie from the peel, tray, or baking sheet right to the wire rack after a minute or so.

Cherry Tomato and Pancetta Pizza

Talk about summery simplicity! Here's a pizza for all basil-and-tomato lovers. Pancetta is cured, not smoked, Italian bacon, often rolled into rounds and used as a flavoring for many stews and braises. Here, it should be diced into ¼-inch cubes so they'll frizzle and turn crunchy when fried.

MAKES 1 PIZZA

Yellow cornmeal to dust the pizza peel or olive oil to grease the pizza tray or the baking sheet

One recipe homemade dough, preferably the Classic Pizza Dough (page 23) or the Semolina Pizza Dough (page 29); or 1 pound purchased fresh dough or frozen dough, thawed; or one 12- to 14-inch store-bought, prebaked plain pizza crust

1 teaspoon olive oil

2 ounces pancetta, diced

6 tablespoons Pizza Pesto (page 40) or purchased pesto

6 ounces mozzarella, shredded

15 cherry tomatoes, halved

1 ounce Parmigiano-Reggiano or Grana Padano, finely grated

BAKING OPTIONS

With a pizza stone. Preheat the stone in the oven at 450°F for 30 to 45 minutes; or preheat the stone on a gas grill at medium, indirect heat (about 450°F) for 30 to 45 minutes; or build an indirect, medium-heat coal bed in a charcoal grill and preheat the stone for the same amount of time.

With a pizza tray or a baking sheet. Preheat the oven to 450°F, a gas grill to indirect, medium heat (about 450°F), or build an indirect, medium-heat fire around the perimeter of a charcoal grill.

CRUST OPTIONS

Fresh dough on a pizza stone. Start out by giving a pizza peel a light dusting with cornmeal. Place the dough at its center; use your fingertips to dimple it into a large circle. Pick it up and shape it with your hands holding its edge, slowly turning the dough until it's about 14 inches in diameter. Set it cornmeal side down on the peel.

Fresh dough on a baking sheet. Grease a pizza tray or a large baking sheet with olive oil dabbed on a paper towel or piece of wax paper. Lay the dough on the tray or baking sheet; dimple it with your fingertips into a rough circle—then pull and press the dough until it forms a circle about 14 inches in diameter on the tray or an irregular rectangle, perhaps 12×7 inches, on the baking sheet.

A prebaked crust. Place it on a pizza peel if you're also using a pizza stone—or place the prebaked crust right on a pizza tray or a large baking sheet.

1. Pour the olive oil into a small skillet and set it over medium heat. Add the pancetta and cook, stirring often, just until the fat has barely begun to turn translucent and the edges are a little sizzled, about 3 minutes. Set aside.

2. Spread the pesto evenly over the crust, leaving a ½-inch border at its edge. Top with the shredded mozzarella.

3. Place the cherry tomatoes cut side up across the pie in a decorative pattern. Sprinkle the diced pancetta over the top, then sprinkle on the grated Parmigiano-Reggiano. Slide the pie from the peel to the hot stone (take care not to dislodge the tomatoes)—or place the pizza on its tray or baking sheet either in the oven or over the portion of the grill grate that's not directly over the heat or coals.

4. Bake or grill with the lid closed until the crust is golden and the pancetta is sizzling and cooked through, 16 to 18 minutes. Use a fork to pop any air bubbles that may spring up at the edges or in the middle of a crust made from fresh dough. Slip the pie back onto the peel to remove it from the stone—or transfer the pie on the tray or baking sheet to a wire rack. Cool for 5 minutes before slicing. If you want to ensure that the crust stays crispy, slip the pizza off the peel, the tray, or the baking sheet after a minute or two, placing it right on the wire rack.

Portobello and Sun-Dried Tomato Pizza

his pizza is perfect for spring or summer: sliced large mushroom caps, some sun-dried tomatoes, and a little cheese. For the best taste without weighing the pie down, use only those sun-dried tomatoes that haven't been packed in oil, most often available in bins in the supermarket's produce section. They should be dry but pliable and still fragrant.

MAKES 1 PIZZA

All-purpose flour for dusting the pizza peel or olive oil for greasing the pizza tray or a large baking sheet

One recipe homemade dough, preferably the Semolina Pizza Dough (page 29); or 1 pound purchased fresh dough or frozen dough, thawed; or one 12- to 14-inch store-bought, prebaked plain pizza crust

10 sun-dried tomatoes (not packed in oil)

⅓ cup Pizza Pesto (page 40) or purchased pesto, preferably of a low-oil variety

2 large portobello mushroom caps, thinly sliced

3 ounces Asiago, finely grated

BAKING OPTIONS

With a pizza stone. Preheat the stone in the oven at 450°F for 30 to 45 minutes; or preheat the stone on a gas grill at medium, indirect heat (about 450°F) for 30 to 45 minutes; or build an indirect, medium-heat coal bed in a charcoal grill and preheat the stone for the same amount of time.

With a pizza tray or a large baking sheet. Preheat the oven to 450°F, a gas grill to indirect, medium heat (about 450°F), or build an indirect, medium-heat coal bed around the perimeter of a charcoal grill.

CRUST OPTIONS

Fresh dough on a pizza stone. First, dust a pizza peel with flour. Add the dough and form it into a large circle by dimpling it with your fingertips. Pick it up and shape it with your hands holding its edge, slowly turning and stretching the dough until it's about 14 inches in diameter. Set it floured side down on the peel.

Fresh dough on a pizza tray or a large baking sheet. Grease the tray or baking sheet with olive oil. Lay the dough on either and dimple the dough with your fingertips until it's a flattened, thick circle—then pull and press the dough until it forms a 14-inch circle on the pizza tray or an irregular 12 × 7-inch rectangle on the baking sheet.

A prebaked crust. Place it on a pizza peel if you're also using a pizza stone—or place the prebaked crust right on a pizza tray or a large baking sheet.

1. Place the sun-dried tomatoes in a bowl, cover with boiling water, and set aside until softened, about 10 minutes.

2. Meanwhile, spread the pesto evenly over the crust, leaving a small border at its edge.

3. Drain the sun-dried tomatoes, cut them into long, thin slices, and arrange these over the pesto. Top with the portobello mushroom slices, then with the grated Asiago.

4. Slip the pizza from the peel to the heated stone—or if you've used a pizza tray or a baking sheet, set either with the pie atop it in the oven or on the unheated portion of the grill grate. Bake or grill with the lid closed until the cheese has melted and turned lightly brown in spots across the pie, 14 to 16 minutes. Slip the peel back under the crust and remove it from the stone—or place the pie on its tray or baking sheet on a wire rack. Cool for 5 minutes before slicing and serving.

Pesto and Dried Cranberry Pizza

This appetizer pie is a marvel of freshness, best with a basil pesto. And easy to boot. Make sure the dried cranberries are plump and juicy to complement the creamy cheese.

MAKES 1 PIZZA

All-purpose flour for dusting the pizza peel or nonstick spray for greasing the pizza tray or a large baking sheet

One recipe homemade dough, preferably the Semolina Pizza Dough (page 29) or the Spelt Pizza Dough (page 33); or 1 pound purchased fresh dough or frozen dough, thawed; or one 12- to 14-inch store-bought, prebaked plain pizza crust

6 tablespoons Pizza Pesto (page 40) or purchased pesto

6 tablespoons chopped dried cranberries

1½ ounces Fontina, shredded

BAKING OPTIONS

With a pizza stone. Preheat the stone in the oven at 450°F for 30 to 45 minutes; or preheat the stone on a gas grill at medium, indirect heat (about 450°F) for 30 to 45 minutes; or build an indirect, medium-heat coal bed in a charcoal grill and preheat the stone for the same amount of time.

With a pizza tray or a large baking sheet. Preheat the oven to 450°F, a gas grill to indirect, medium heat (about 450°F), or build an indirect, medium-heat fire around the perimeter of a charcoal grill.

CRUST OPTIONS

Fresh dough on a pizza stone. First, dust a pizza peel with flour; set the dough at its center. Form the dough into a flattened, large circle by dimpling it with your fingertips. Pick it up and shape it with your hands, holding its edge, slowly turning the dough and gently stretching it until it's about 14 inches in diameter. If you're working with the Spelt Pizza Dough, it's too fragile to hold up in the air and shape; see page 34 for special instructions. In any event, set the shaped dough floured side down on the peel.

Fresh dough on a pizza tray or a large baking sheet. Grease the tray or baking sheet with nonstick spray. Lay the dough at the center of either and dimple the dough with your fingertips, flattening it as you do so—then pull and press it until it forms a 14-inch circle on the pizza tray or an irregular 12×7-inch rectangle on the baking sheet.

A prebaked crust. Place it on a floured pizza peel if you're also using a pizza stone—or place the prebaked crust right on a pizza tray or a large baking sheet.

1. Spread the pesto over the prepared crust, leaving a ½-inch border at the perimeter. Top with the chopped dried cranberries, then the shredded Fontina.

2. Slide the pie from the peel to the very hot stone or place the pie on its tray or baking sheet either in the oven or on the grill grate over the unheated portion. Bake or grill with the lid closed until the cheese has melted and the crust is somewhat firm to the touch, even darkened a bit on its bottom, 16 to 18 minutes. Slide the peel back under the pie to remove it from the very hot stone or transfer the pizza on the tray or the baking sheet to a wire rack. Cool for 5 minutes before slicing.

Fig and Prosciutto Pizza

We first encountered a pie like this one at the best pizza parlor in Massachusetts, if not in all of New England: Babba Louie's in Great Barrington. Wait until fresh figs are in season before making this over-the-top indulgence.

MAKES 1 PIZZA

Yellow cornmeal for dusting a pizza peel or olive oil for greasing a pizza tray or a large baking sheet

One recipe homemade dough, preferably the Whole Wheat Pizza Dough (page 25); or 1 pound purchased fresh dough or frozen dough, thawed; or one 12- to 14-inch store-bought, prebaked plain pizza crust

2 tablespoons olive oil

12 ounces (¾ pound) broccoli rabe, chopped (about 2 cups)

2 garlic cloves, minced

6 tablespoons Classic Pizza Sauce (page 38), No-Cook Pizza Sauce (page 39), or jarred plain pizza sauce

6 ounces mozzarella, shredded

3 ounces thinly sliced prosciutto, chopped

3 fresh, ripe figs, quartered

1 to 2 ounces Gorgonzola or Danish blue, crumbled

2 tablespoons minced fresh rosemary

½ teaspoon freshly ground black pepper

BAKING OPTIONS

With a pizza stone. Preheat the stone in the oven at 450°F for 30 to 45 minutes; or preheat the stone on a gas grill at medium, indirect heat (about 450°F) for 30 to 45 minutes; or build an indirect, medium-heat coal bed in a charcoal grill and preheat the stone for the same amount of time.

With a pizza tray or a large baking sheet. Preheat the oven to 450°F, a gas grill to indirect, medium heat (about 450°F), or build an indirect, medium-heat coal bed around the perimeter of a charcoal grill.

CRUST OPTIONS

Fresh dough on a pizza stone. Dust a pizza peel with cornmeal, then set the dough at its center. Dimple the dough into a flattened circle, using your fingertips. Hold it by its edge and pick it up, then turn and stretch it until it's a circle about 14 inches in diameter. Set the dough cornmeal side down on the peel.

Fresh dough on a pizza tray or a large baking sheet. Grease either with some olive oil dabbed on a paper towel or on a piece of wax paper. Lay the dough on the pizza tray or the baking sheet; dimple the dough with your fingertips until it's a flattened circle—then pull and press that circle until it forms one about 14 inches in diameter on the tray or an irregular 12 × 7-inch rectangle on the baking sheet.

A prebaked crust. Place it on a cornmeal dusted pizza peel if you're also using a pizza stone—or place the prebaked crust right on a pizza tray or a large baking sheet.

1. Heat a large skillet over medium heat, then swirl in the olive oil. Add the broccoli rabe; sauté until wilted, about 4 minutes. Add the garlic and continue cooking, stirring often, until tender, about 4 more minutes.

2. Spread the pizza sauce evenly over the crust, leaving a ½-inch border at its perimeter. Top the sauce with the shredded mozzarella.

3. Spoon the broccoli rabe and garlic over the pizza, then top with the prosciutto and fig quarters. Sprinkle the blue cheese, rosemary, and the black pepper over the pie.

4. Slide the pizza from the peel to the heated stone; if you've used a pizza tray or a baking sheet, set it in the oven on the middle rack or place it over the unheated portion of the grill. Bake or grill with the lid closed until the cheese has melted, the sauce is hot, and the crust has begun to firm up, 16 to 18 minutes. Slide the peel back under the crust on the very hot stone to remove it and cool it for 5 minutes, or transfer the pie on its tray or baking sheet to a wire rack to cool the pie for 5 minutes before slicing and serving.

Smoked Salmon Pizza

Don't cook the smoked salmon or it will turn oily and unappealing. Arrange the salmon on top of the baked pie just before it's ready to be sliced and served.

MAKES 1 PIZZA

All-purpose flour for the pizza peel or nonstick spray for the pizza tray or the baking sheet

One recipe homemade dough, preferably the Classic Pizza Dough (page 23); or 1 pound purchased fresh dough or frozen dough, thawed; or one 12- to 14-inch store-bought, prebaked plain pizza crust

1 tablespoon olive oil

4 medium shallots, thinly sliced

½ teaspoon freshly ground black pepper

¼ cup regular, low-fat, or fat-free sour cream

2 tablespoons regular, low-fat, or fat-free cream cheese, at room temperature

1 tablespoon capers, drained and rinsed

1 tablespoon chopped fresh dill or 1 teaspoon dried dill

2 teaspoons lemon juice

4 ounces thinly sliced smoked salmon

BAKING OPTIONS

With a pizza stone. Preheat the stone in the oven at 400°F for 45 minutes (note the slightly lower temperature than is usually called for in this book); or preheat the stone on a gas grill at medium, indirect heat (about 400°F) for about 45 minutes; or build an indirect, medium-heat coal bed in a charcoal grill and preheat the stone for the same amount of time.

With a pizza tray or a large baking sheet. Preheat the oven to 400°F (again, note the slightly lower temperature), a gas grill to indirect, medium heat (about

400°F), or build an indirect, medium-heat coal bed around the perimeter of a charcoal grill.

CRUST OPTIONS

Fresh dough on a pizza stone. Dust a pizza peel with flour; set the dough at its center. Form the dough into a large, flat circle by dimpling it with your fingertips. Pick it up and shape it by holding its edge and slowly rotating it, stretching the edge all the while, until it's about 14 inches in diameter. Set it floured side down on the peel.

Fresh dough on a pizza tray or a large baking sheet. Grease the tray or baking sheet with nonstick spray. Lay the dough at the center and dimple it into a flattened circle with your fingertips—then pull and press it until it forms a circle about 14 inches in diameter on the tray or a 12 × 7-inch somewhat irregular rectangle on the baking sheet.

A prebaked crust. Place it on a floured pizza peel if you're also using a pizza stone—or place the prebaked crust on a pizza tray or a large baking sheet.

1. Spread the olive oil evenly over the crust, then top with the shallots, leaving a ½-inch border around the perimeter of the pie. Sprinkle with black pepper.

2. Slide the crust from the peel to the hot stone or place the pie on the tray or baking sheet either in the oven or over the unheated section of the grill rack. Bake or grill with the lid closed, until the crust is golden brown and somewhat firm to the touch, 14 to 16 minutes. If you're working with fresh dough, you'll need to pop any air bubbles that form at its edge or across its surface, particularly during the first 10 minutes. Slide the peel back under the crust to get it off the stone (watch out: that stone is very hot)—or transfer the pie on its tray or baking sheet to a wire rack. Cool the crust on the peel or the baking sheet for 5 minutes.

3. Whisk the sour cream, cream cheese, capers, dill, and lemon juice in a small bowl until creamy and spreadable.

4. Spread this mixture evenly over the warm crust, taking care not to dislodge the roasted shallots and keeping that ½-inch border intact. Lay the smoked salmon pieces evenly over the pizza, then slice and serve.

Tuna and White Bean Pizza

This pizza is a takeoff on the classic, summery bruschetta, a great starter. Look for Italian tuna packed in olive oil, often available at specialty Italian markets and online sites; the pizza will be so much better.

MAKES 1 PIZZA

Yellow cornmeal for dusting the pizza peel or olive oil for greasing the pizza tray or the baking sheet

One recipe homemade dough, preferably the Olive Oil Pizza Dough (page 27); or 1 pound purchased fresh dough or frozen dough, thawed; or one 12- to 14-inch store-bought, prebaked plain pizza crust

1¼ cups canned white beans, rinsed and drained

One 7-ounce can tuna packed in olive oil, drained

3 tablespoons minced sage leaves, or parsley leaves, or oregano leaves, or stemmed thyme leaves, or a combination of any two herbs to equal 3 tablespoons

3 ounces Parmigiano-Reggiano or Grana Padano, shaved into thin strips

2 tablespoons extra virgin olive oil

½ medium lemon

BAKING OPTIONS

With a pizza stone. Preheat the stone in the oven at 450°F for 30 to 45 minutes; or preheat the stone on a gas grill at medium, indirect heat (about 450°F) for 30 to 45 minutes; or build an indirect, medium-heat coal bed in a charcoal grill and preheat the stone for the same amount of time.

With a pizza tray or a large baking sheet. Preheat the oven to 450°F, a gas grill to indirect, medium heat (about 450°F), or build an indirect, medium-heat fire around the perimeter of a charcoal grill.

CRUST OPTIONS

Fresh dough on a pizza stone. First, dust a pizza peel lightly with cornmeal. Set the dough on the peel and form the dough into a large circle by dimpling it with your fingertips. Pick it up, hold its edge in both hands, and rotate it, slowly but gently stretching the edge all the while, until the circle is about 14 inches in diameter. Set the dough cornmeal side down on the peel.

Fresh dough on a pizza tray or a large baking sheet. Grease the tray or baking sheet with some olive oil dabbed on a paper towel. Lay the dough at the center of either and dimple the dough into a flat, thick circle with your fingertips—then pull and press it until it forms a circle about 14 inches in diameter on the pizza tray or an irregular rectangle, about 12 × 7 inches, on the baking sheet.

A prebaked crust. Place it on a cornmeal-dusted pizza peel if you're also using a pizza stone—or place the prebaked crust on a pizza tray or a large baking sheet.

1. Mix the beans, tuna, and minced herb in a medium bowl. Spread evenly over the prepared crust, leaving a ½-inch border at its edge.

2. Top with the shaved cheese, then drizzle the extra virgin olive oil over the pie. Slip it from the peel to the very hot stone or place the tray or the baking sheet holding the pizza either in the oven or over the portion of the grill grate that is not directly over the heat or the coals.

3. Bake or grill until the crust is golden brown and even a little darkened on its bottom side, 16 to 18 minutes. Being careful not to dislodge the toppings, slip the peel back under the crust to remove it from the stone—or transfer the tray or the baking sheet with its pie to a wire rack.

4. Squeeze the lemon over the pizza, taking care to catch the seeds. It helps to squeeze the lemon through a strainer or into your cleaned palm where the juice can run between your fingers while the seeds stay in your palm. Set the pie aside to cool for 5 minutes before slicing.

Corn Relish and Roasted Garlic Pizza

his pizza is crafted from the ingredients for corn relish—with the addition of roasted garlic to give the flavors some heft. If you want a little more zip, drizzle the pie with 1 tablespoon white wine vinegar the moment it comes off the grill or out of the oven.

MAKES 1 PIZZA

Yellow cornmeal for dusting the pizza peel or olive oil for greasing the pizza tray or the large baking sheet

One recipe homemade dough, preferably the Parmesan Pizza Dough (page 31) or the Cracker Pizza Dough (page 35); or 1 pound purchased fresh dough or frozen dough, thawed; or one 12- to 14-inch store-bought, prebaked plain pizza crust

1 garlic head

1 cup fresh or frozen corn kernels (see Note)

1 jarred roasted red pepper, diced—or see steps 1 and 2 of Chorizo and Red Pepper Pizza (page 210) for how to roast a red bell pepper

2 tablespoons chopped fresh rosemary

¼ teaspoon salt

8 ounces (½ pound) Monterey Jack, shredded

1 jarred whole jalapeño, seeded and minced

BAKING OPTIONS

With a pizza stone. Preheat the stone in the oven at 450°F for 30 to 45 minutes; or preheat the stone on a gas grill at medium, indirect heat (about 450°F) for 30 to 45 minutes; or build an indirect, medium-heat coal bed in a charcoal grill and preheat the stone for the same amount of time.

With a pizza tray or a large baking sheet. Preheat the oven to 450°F, a gas grill to indirect, medium heat (about 450°F), or build an indirect, medium-heat coal bed around the perimeter of a charcoal grill.

CRUST OPTIONS

Fresh dough on a pizza stone. Start out by dusting a pizza peel with cornmeal and then setting the dough in its center. Use your fingertips to dimple the dough into a large, thick, rippled circle. Then pick it up and shape it by rotating it from its edge, holding it with your hands at about ten and two o'clock, until the dough is a circle about 14 inches in diameter. The Cracker Pizza Dough will not stand up to being held as it's shaped—see page 35 for more details. In any case, set the shaped dough cornmeal side down on the peel.

Fresh dough on a pizza tray or a baking sheet. Grease a pizza tray or a large baking sheet with olive oil dabbed on a paper towel. Lay the dough on the tray or the baking sheet; dimple it with your fingertips until it's a thick, flattened circle. Then pull and press the dough until it forms a 14-inch circle on the tray or an irregular rectangle, about 12 × 7 inches, on the baking sheet.

A prebaked crust. Place it on a cornmeal-dusted pizza peel if you're also using a pizza stone—or place the prebaked crust right on a pizza tray or a large baking sheet.

1. Cut the top third off the garlic head, exposing the cloves. Wrap the head in aluminum foil and bake in the preheated oven or on the grill over direct heat until the cloves are quite soft, 30 to 35 minutes. Cool for 10 minutes.

2. Mix the corn, roasted red pepper, rosemary, and salt in a medium bowl.

3. Sprinkle the shredded Monterey Jack evenly over the crust, leaving a ½-inch space at the perimeter that is not coated. Unwrap the garlic and squeeze the cloves out onto a cutting board. Chop them into quarters, then dot these across the pie. Top with the corn mixture, then sprinkle with the minced jalapeño.

4. Slide the pizza from the peel to the hot stone—or if you've used a pizza tray or a baking sheet, place it either in the oven or over the unheated portion of the grill grate. Bake or grill with the lid closed until the cheese has melted underneath the corn and the crust has begun to turn a golden brown, 16 to 18 minutes. If using fresh dough, check it once in a while, particularly during the first 10 minutes, to pop any air bubbles that may rise up on its edge or even in its middle. Slip the peel under the baked pizza to take it off the stone and set aside—or transfer the pizza tray or the baking sheet to a wire cooling rack. Cool for 5 minutes before slicing.

NOTE: To remove corn kernels off a cob, slice off one end so the cob will stand up straight on a cutting board. Run a sharp knife down the cob, shearing off the kernels while staying fairly close to the cob. Two medium ears will yield about 1 cup kernels.

Watermelon Pizza

We first had a version of this pie at Gonzo's, a Venetian-style restaurant in New York's Greenwich Village. The watermelon chunks should be quite cold so that they make a nice contrast to the melted cheese on top. Make sure you buy seedless watermelon.

MAKES 1 PIZZA

Either all-purpose flour for dusting the pizza peel or nonstick spray for greasing the pizza tray or the baking sheet

One recipe homemade dough, preferably the Classic Pizza Dough (page 23) or the Cracker Pizza Dough (page 35); or 1 pound purchased fresh dough or frozen dough, thawed; or one 12- to 14-inch store-bought, prebaked plain pizza crust

8 ounces (½ pound) Brie, rind removed and at room temperature (see Note)

2 cups diced, cold, seedless watermelon

3 tablespoons minced basil leaves

2 ounces Parmigiano-Reggiano, shaved into thin strips

½ teaspoon freshly ground black pepper

BAKING OPTIONS

With a pizza stone. Preheat the stone in the oven at 450°F for 30 to 45 minutes; or preheat the stone on a gas grill at medium, indirect heat (about 450°F) for 30 to 45 minutes; or build an indirect, medium-heat coal bed in a charcoal grill and preheat the stone for the same amount of time.

With a pizza tray or a large baking sheet. Preheat the oven to 450°F, a gas grill to indirect, medium heat (about 450°F), or build an indirect, medium-heat coal bed around the perimeter of a charcoal grill.

CRUST OPTIONS

Fresh dough on a pizza stone. First, dust a pizza peel with flour. Add the dough and form it into a large circle by dimpling it with your fingertips. Pick up the dough and shape it by holding its edge, slowly rotating it and stretching that edge, until the circle is about 14 inches in diameter. The Cracker Pizza Dough is not sturdy enough to withstand much pulling; see page 35 for special instructions related to its shaping. Set the dough floured side down on the peel.

Fresh dough on a pizza tray or a large baking sheet. Grease the tray or baking sheet with nonstick spray. Lay the dough at the center; dimple the dough into a flat, thick circle with your fingertips—then pull and press it until it forms a 14-inch circle or an irregular 12 × 7-inch rectangle on the baking sheet.

A prebaked crust. Place it on a pizza peel if you're also using a pizza stone—or place the prebaked crust right on a pizza tray or a large baking sheet.

1. Slip the prepared dough from the peel to the hot stone or place the dough on its tray or baking sheet either in the oven or on the portion of the grill grate that's not directly over the heat or coals. Bake or grill with the lid closed until lightly browned, about 12 minutes.

2. Slip the peel back under the crust to remove it from the stone or transfer the crust on its tray or baking sheet to a wire rack. Cool for 5 minutes.

3. Spread the softened Brie evenly over the crust, leaving about $\frac{1}{2}$ inch at the perimeter. Return the crust to the stone, the oven, or the grate that's not directly over the heat. Bake or grill with the lid closed until the cheese has melted, about 5 minutes. Again, slip the peel under the pizza to take it off the stone or transfer the pie on its tray or baking sheet to a wire rack.

4. Preheat the oven's broiler, setting the rack 4 to 6 inches from the heat source. If you're working with a pizza stone, you'll now need to transfer the crust from the peel to a large baking sheet.

5. Top the pie with the diced watermelon and the minced basil. Then lay the Parmigiano-Reggiano strips evenly over the watermelon slices. Sprinkle the pie with the black pepper.

6. Set the pizza on its baking sheet under the broiler and broil until the Parmigiano-Reggiano begins to melt, about 3 minutes. Transfer the pie on the baking sheet to a wire rack and cool for 5 minutes before slicing.

NOTE: It's easiest to remove the top and side rind from the Brie while the cheese is still cold from the refrigerator; then let it sit out to come to room temperature for about 1 hour. Scoop the soft cheese off the bottom rind to spread it on the prepared crust.

Focaccia, Pizza Style

No, a pizza dough will not give you the classic Italian flatbread—but it will make a quick alternative, an excellent snack with cocktails or wine. Use only fresh dough for this recipe and note the slightly higher baking temperature.

MAKES 1 FLATBREAD APPETIZER

Either yellow cornmeal to dust a pizza peel or olive oil to grease a pizza tray or a large baking sheet

One recipe homemade dough, preferably the Classic Pizza Dough (page 23) or the Olive Oil Pizza Dough (page 27); or 1 pound purchased fresh dough or frozen dough, thawed

2 tablespoons extra virgin olive oil

2 garlic cloves, minced

2 plum or Roma tomatoes, thinly sliced

½ teaspoon salt, preferably coarse kosher salt

¼ teaspoon freshly ground black pepper

BAKING OPTIONS

With a pizza stone. Preheat the stone in the oven at 475°F for 30 to 45 minutes; or preheat the stone on a gas grill at medium-high, indirect heat (about 500°F) for 30 to 45 minutes; or build an indirect, medium-high heat coal bed in a charcoal grill and preheat the stone for the same amount of time.

With a pizza tray or a large baking sheet. Preheat the oven to 475°F, a gas grill to indirect, medium-high heat (about 500°F), or build an indirect, medium-heat coal bed around the perimeter of a charcoal grill.

CRUST OPTIONS

Fresh dough on a pizza stone. Dust a pizza peel with cornmeal, then place the dough at its center. Dimple the dough into a flattened circle with your fingertips. Pick it up and shape it with your hands, holding its edge, slowly turning the dough until it's a circle about 14 inches in diameter. Set it cornmeal side down on the peel.

Fresh dough on a pizza tray or a large baking sheet. Grease the tray or baking sheet with some olive oil on a paper towel. Lay the dough on the tray or baking sheet; dimple the dough with your fingertips—then pull and press the dough until it forms a 14-inch circle on the tray or a 12 × 7-inch irregular rectangle on the baking sheet.

1. Brush the olive oil over the crust, then sprinkle the minced garlic evenly over the top.

2. Lay the sliced tomatoes in a decorative pattern over the crust, keeping them ½ inch back from the edge. Sprinkle with salt and pepper.

3. Slip the pie from the peel to the heated stone or place the pie on its tray or baking sheet in the oven or on the grill over indirect heat. Bake or grill with the lid closed until the tomatoes have dried out a bit and the crust is lightly browned and crunchy, 12 to 14 minutes. Slip the peel back under the crust to remove it from the stone and cool the pizza for 5 minutes, or transfer the pie on its tray or baking sheet to a wire rack and cool for 5 minutes before slicing into squares or rectangles.

Pissaladière, Pizza Style

Although not authentic, this is an easy pizza version of the south-of-France favorite: a thick bread crust topped with black olives, anchovies, and caramelized onions. Look for cipollini, tiny Italian onions, in the produce section of well-stocked supermarkets; or forgo roasting the onions and buy them preroasted from the supermarket salad bar.

MAKES 1 PIZZA

Either all-purpose flour for the pizza peel or olive oil for the pizza tray or the baking sheet
One recipe homemade dough, preferably the Olive Oil Pizza Dough (page 27); or 1 pound purchased fresh dough or frozen dough, thawed; or one 12- to 14-inch store-bought, prebaked plain pizza crust
8 ounces (½ pound) cipollini, peeled
2 tablespoons olive oil
3 ounces tinned anchovy fillets (about 20)
18 pitted black olives
1½ ounces Parmigiano-Reggiano, finely grated

BAKING OPTIONS

With a pizza stone. Preheat the stone in the oven at 450°F for 30 to 45 minutes; or preheat the stone on a gas grill at medium, indirect heat (about 450°F) for 30 to 45 minutes; or build an indirect, medium-heat coal bed in a charcoal grill and preheat the stone for the same amount of time.

With a pizza tray or a large baking sheet. Preheat the oven to 450°F, a gas grill to indirect, medium heat (about 450°F), or build an indirect, medium-heat fire around the perimeter of a charcoal grill.

CRUST OPTIONS

Fresh dough on a pizza stone. First, dust a pizza peel with flour. Set the dough at its center and form the dough into a large, flattened circle by dimpling it with your fingertips. Pick it up and shape it by pulling and stretching it from its edge until it's about 14 inches in diameter. Set the shaped dough floured side down on the peel.

Fresh dough on a pizza tray or a large baking sheet. Grease either one with a little olive oil. Lay the dough on either and dimple the dough with your fingertips until it's a flattened circle—then pull and press the dough until it forms a 14-inch circle on the pizza tray or an irregular rectangle, about 12×7 inches, on the baking sheet.

A prebaked crust. Place it on a pizza peel if you're also using a floured pizza stone—or place the prebaked crust on a pizza tray or a large baking sheet.

1. Toss the onions with the olive oil in a 9- or 10-inch baking pan and roast in the preheated oven or directly over the heat on the preheated grill, stirring occasionally, until tender and golden, about 50 minutes in the oven or about 35 minutes on the grill. (If roasting on the grill, the baking pan must be flame-safe.)

2. Transfer the onions to a cutting board, cool slightly, and chop. Spread the chopped onions over the prepared crust, leaving a ½-inch border at its edge.

3. Lay the anchovy fillets and olives in a decorative pattern over the crust. Top with the grated Parmigiano-Reggiano.

4. Slide the crust from the peel to the hot stone or place the pizza on its tray or baking sheet either in the oven or over the portion of the grill grate that's not directly over the heat source. Bake or grill with the lid closed until the crust is lightly browned and somewhat firm, 14 to 16 minutes. If working with fresh dough, pop any air bubbles that may arise across its surface or at its edge to yield an even crust. Slide the peel back under the crust to get it off the hot stone or transfer the pizza on its tray or baking sheet to a wire rack. Set aside to cool for 5 minutes before slicing and serving. To make sure the crust stays crunchy, transfer the pie from the peel, tray, or baking sheet directly to the wire rack after a minute or so.

FIVE SALAD PIZZAS

Tossed Salad Pizza 119

Spinach Salad Pizza 122

BLT Pizza 125

Chicken Caesar Salad Pizza 128

Steak and Arugula Pizza 131

T hese pies are topped with fresh salad. The dressed greens are not grilled or baked; rather, they are placed on top of a hot pie, a wonderful combination of cold and hot, of fresh and baked.

Salad pizzas succeed based on the freshness of the salad greens. Pick them over to make sure you get rid of any wilted, soggy, or rusted leaves. If at all possible, buy those greens in heads—or at least in containers that let them have plenty of aeration and plenty of space to move around so they don't get crushed or gooey.

If you buy fresh lettuces still on the heads, wash them well to get rid of any sand or grit between the leaves. Fill a cleaned sink with cool water, then plunge the individual leaves into it. Soak for 3 to 5 minutes, stirring once or twice, to let any dirt fall to the bottom of the sink. Remove carefully without draining the water, washing off individual leaves if any are still dirty. Once all the greens are out of the sink, drain the water and wash away the grit. Then whirl the leaves in a salad spinner or gently dab them dry between generous layers of paper towels.

Tossed Salad Pizza

Plain and simple—a good pie for lunch or dinner anytime. For the best salad, don't just use a wad of cloyingly soft greens, such as those found in the ever-prevalent mesclun mix. Rather, combine softer greens like mizuna or mâche with some crunchy romaine or peppery curly endive. Note the slightly lower oven or grill temperature so that the barely topped crust doesn't burn.

MAKES 1 PIZZA

Either yellow cornmeal for the pizza peel or olive oil for the pizza tray or the baking sheet

One recipe homemade dough, preferably the Classic Pizza Dough (page 23); or 1 pound purchased fresh dough or frozen dough, thawed; or one 12- to 14-inch store-bought, prebaked plain pizza crust

3 tablespoons olive oil

1 medium red onion, thinly sliced

3 garlic cloves, minced

2 ounces Parmigiano-Reggiano, shaved

½ teaspoon freshly ground black pepper

1 tablespoon white wine vinegar

1 teaspoon Dijon mustard

1 teaspoon tahini

1 teaspoon lemon juice

¼ teaspoon salt

4 cups mixed salad greens

½ medium cucumber, peeled, halved lengthwise, seeded, and thinly sliced

BAKING OPTIONS

With a pizza stone. Preheat the stone in the oven at 400°F for 30 to 45 minutes; or preheat the stone on a gas grill at medium, indirect heat (about 400°F) for 30

to 45 minutes; or build an indirect, medium-heat coal bed in a charcoal grill and preheat the stone for the same amount of time.

With a baking sheet. Preheat the oven to 400°F, a gas grill to indirect, medium heat (about 400°F), or build an indirect, medium-heat fire around the perimeter of a charcoal grill.

CRUST OPTIONS

Fresh dough on a pizza stone. Dust a pizza peel with cornmeal. Add the dough and form it into a large circle by dimpling it with your fingertips. Pick up the dough and shape it by holding its edge in both hands and rotating it, slowly stretching the edge, until the circle is about 14 inches in diameter. Set it cornmeal side down on the peel.

Fresh dough on a pizza tray or a large baking sheet. Grease the tray or baking sheet with some olive oil. Lay the dough at the center of either and dimple the dough into a flat, thick circle with your fingertips, then pull and press it until it forms a 14-inch circle on the tray or an irregular 12 × 7-inch rectangle on the baking sheet.

A prebaked crust. Place it on a pizza peel if using a pizza stone—or place the prebaked crust on a pizza tray or a large baking sheet.

1. Spread 1 tablespoon of the olive oil evenly over the crust, then lay the red onion slices over it, keeping a ½-inch border at the edge.

2. Top with the minced garlic, then lay the strips of Parmigiano-Reggiano over the pie. Sprinkle with the pepper.

3. Slide the topped crust from the peel to the heated stone or place the pie on its tray or baking sheet either in the oven or over the unheated section of the grill grate. Bake or grill with the lid closed until the crust is lightly browned and somewhat firm to the touch, 14 to 16 minutes. If working with fresh dough, take care during the first 10 minutes to pop any air bubbles that might arise on its surface.

4. Slide the peel back under the crust to get it off the very hot stone or transfer the pie on its tray or baking sheet to a wire cooling rack. Cool for 5 minutes. To ensure a crunchy crust, transfer it directly to the wire rack after a minute or two.

5. Whisk the vinegar, mustard, tahini, lemon juice, and salt in a large bowl until smooth. Whisk in the remaining 2 tablespoons olive oil in a slow, steady stream until the mixture is creamy.

6. Add the greens and cucumber; toss well to coat. Mound this dressed salad over the baked crust, then slice into wedges to serve.

Spinach Salad Pizza

traditional spinach salad laced with bacon tops this pie. For the best taste, use baby spinach leaves, not the larger, leafier variety.

MAKES 1 PIZZA

All-purpose flour to dust the pizza peel or olive oil to grease the pizza tray or a large baking sheet

One recipe homemade dough, preferably the Semolina Pizza Dough (page 29); or 1 pound purchased fresh dough or frozen dough, thawed; or one 12- to 14-inch store-bought, prebaked plain pizza crust

8 ounces (½ pound) pork, turkey, or soy bacon, chopped

1 small yellow onion, chopped (about ½ cup)

8 ounces (½ pound) cremini mushrooms, cleaned and thinly sliced

½ teaspoon salt

½ teaspoon freshly ground black pepper

¼ teaspoon ground cloves

¼ teaspoon garlic powder

5 ounces soft goat cheese, crumbled

Up to 2 tablespoons extra virgin olive oil

2 tablespoons balsamic vinegar

2 cups packed baby spinach leaves

BAKING OPTIONS

With a pizza stone. Position the rack in the middle of the oven and preheat the stone in the oven at 400°F for 30 to 45 minutes; or preheat the stone on a gas grill at medium, indirect heat (about 400°F) for 30 to 45 minutes; or build an indirect, medium-heat coal bed in a charcoal grill and then preheat the stone for the same amount of time.

With a pizza tray or a baking sheet. Preheat the oven to 400°F, a gas grill to indirect, medium heat (about 400°F), or build an indirect, medium-heat coal bed around the perimeter of a charcoal grill.

CRUST OPTIONS

Fresh dough on a pizza stone. Dust a pizza peel with flour, set the dough at its center, and form the dough into a large, flat circle by dimpling it with your fingertips. Pick it up, hold it by the edge with both hands, and slowly rotate the dough, stretching its edge gently, until the circle is about 14 inches in diameter. Place the dough floured side down on the peel.

Fresh dough on a pizza tray or a large baking sheet. Grease one or the other with some olive oil on a piece of paper towel. Lay the dough at the center of either; dimple the dough with your fingertips, then pull and press it until it forms a 14-inch circle on the tray or an irregular rectangle, about 12 × 7 inches, on the baking sheet.

A prebaked crust. Place it on a floured pizza peel if using a pizza stone—or place the prebaked crust on a pizza tray or a large baking sheet.

1. Fry the bacon in a large skillet over medium heat, stirring frequently, until lightly browned but not too crisp (it will continue to cook as the pizza bakes or grills), about 4 minutes. Transfer to a plate using a slotted spoon.

2. Add the onion to the skillet (still over medium heat) and cook, stirring frequently, until softened, about 3 minutes.

3. Add the mushrooms and cook, stirring often, until they give off their liquid and it evaporates to a glaze, about 5 minutes.

4. Return the bacon pieces to the skillet. Add the salt, pepper, cloves, and garlic powder. Stir well, then use a slotted spoon to transfer this mixture and spread it evenly over the prepared crust, leaving a ½-inch border at its edge. (Do not throw out the bacon drippings in the skillet.)

5. Sprinkle the cheese over the crust, remembering to keep that ½-inch border at the edge. Slip the crust from the peel onto the stone or place the pie on its tray or baking sheet in the oven or on the grill. Bake or grill with the lid closed until the crust is lightly browned and firm at its edge, about 18 minutes. If using fresh dough, check it occasionally to pop any air bubbles that form across its surface.

6. Meanwhile, set the skillet with the bacon drippings over medium heat; add enough olive oil that the amount of fat comes up to about 3 tablespoons. Heat well, perhaps 2 minutes; then remove from the heat and stir in the vinegar, scraping up any browned bits on the skillet's bottom. Set aside, covered, on the back of the stove to keep warm.

7. Slip the peel back under the crust and remove it from the stone, or transfer the pie on its tray or baking sheet to a wire rack. Set aside to cool for 5 minutes. If desired, transfer the pizza right onto the wire rack after a minute or so.

8. Mound the spinach leaves on top of the pie, then drizzle the skillet dressing evenly over the pie before slicing and serving.

BLT Pizza

S alad pies are best eaten with a knife and fork—and that's certainly true of this riff on the diner classic. Use only iceberg lettuce: it's got the perfect crunch for this simple pie.

MAKES 1 PIZZA

All-purpose flour to dust the pizza peel or nonstick spray to grease the pizza tray or the baking sheet

One recipe homemade dough, preferably the Classic Pizza Dough (page 23); or the Cracker Pizza Dough (page 35); or 1 pound purchased fresh dough or frozen dough, thawed; or one 12- to 14-inch store-bought, prebaked plain pizza crust

12 ounces (¾ pound) pork, beef, turkey, or soy bacon strips

1½ tablespoons plus 1 teaspoon Dijon or honey mustard

6 ounces mozzarella, shredded

1 large beefsteak tomato, seeded and diced (see Notes)

2 tablespoons regular, low-fat, or fat-free mayonnaise

2 teaspoons lemon juice

1 teaspoon Worcestershire sauce

2 cups shredded, packed iceberg lettuce (about half a large head; see Notes)

BAKING OPTIONS

With a pizza stone. Preheat the stone in the oven at 450°F for 30 to 45 minutes; or preheat the stone on a gas grill at medium, indirect heat (about 450°F) for 30 to 45 minutes; or build an indirect, medium-heat coal bed in a charcoal grill and preheat the stone for the same amount of time.

With a pizza tray or a large baking sheet. Preheat the oven to 450°F, a gas grill to indirect, medium heat (about 450°F), or build an indirect, medium-heat fire around the perimeter of a charcoal grill.

CRUST OPTIONS

Fresh dough on a pizza stone. Lightly dust a pizza peel with flour. Add the dough and form it into a large circle by dimpling it with your fingertips. Pick up the dough and shape it by holding it at the edge and slowly rotating and stretching it until it's a circle about 14 inches in diameter. Set the crust floured side down on the peel.

Fresh dough on a pizza tray or a large baking sheet. Grease either with nonstick spray. Lay the dough on the tray or baking sheet, then dimple it with your fingertips. Pull and press the dough until it forms a 14-inch circle on the sheet or an irregular rectangle, about 12×7 inches, on the baking sheet.

A prebaked crust. Place it on a pizza peel if you're also using a pizza stone—or place the prebaked crust right on a pizza tray or large baking sheet.

1. Fry the bacon strips in a large skillet over medium heat until just starting to turn brown, turning occasionally, about 3 minutes. Remove the strips from the skillet and cut into 1-inch pieces. Set aside.

2. Spread 1½ tablespoons mustard over the crust, leaving a ½-inch border at its edge. Sprinkle the shredded mozzarella evenly over the mustard, then top with the diced tomato and the chopped bacon.

3. Slip the crust from the peel to the very hot stone. If you've put the pie on a pizza tray or a large baking sheet, slip it right into the oven or set it over the unheated portion of the grill. Bake or grill with the lid closed until the bacon is crispy and the crust is golden, 16 to 18 minutes.

4. Slip the crust back onto the peel, taking care of that very hot stone—or transfer the pizza tray or the baking sheet with its pie to a wire rack. In either case, set the pizza aside for 5 minutes to cool slightly. For a crisper crust, carefully transfer the pizza from the peel, tray, or baking sheet to a wire rack after about 1 minute.

5. Meanwhile, whisk the mayonnaise, lemon juice, Worcestershire sauce, and the remaining 1 teaspoon mustard in a large bowl until smooth.

6. Add the lettuce and toss until well coated. Mound the dressed salad onto the pizza, then cut into wedges to serve.

NOTES: To seed a tomato, cut it into quarters, then gently squeeze the pieces over the sink, running your finger into the chambers to release the seed pockets and their juice.

To shred the lettuce, cut the head in half through the stem end. Lay one half cut side down on a cutting board and make very thin slices through the lettuce, starting at the side opposite the core. Pull these lettuce bits apart to shred them into long threads.

Chicken Caesar Salad Pizza

Chicken Caesar salad has become a staple at home and in restaurants. We think it should become a pizza topping, too. The dressing uses a raw egg yolk for the classic taste. Use only organic eggs and know your producer—and the risks. If you have any doubts, leave out the egg yolk and increase the olive oil to ¼ cup.

MAKES 1 PIZZA

All-purpose flour to dust a pizza peel or olive oil to grease a pizza tray or a baking sheet

One recipe homemade dough, preferably the Semolina Pizza Dough (page 29) or the Parmesan Pizza Dough (page 31); or 1 pound purchased fresh dough or frozen dough, thawed; or one 12- to 14-inch store-bought, prebaked plain pizza crust

Nonstick spray

8 ounces (½ pound) boneless skinless chicken breasts

1½ tablespoons honey mustard

3 ounces mozzarella, finely grated through the small holes of a box grater

1 small red bell pepper, seeded and finely chopped

1 garlic clove, minced

2 anchovy fillets

½ teaspoon salt

½ teaspoon freshly ground black pepper

1 large egg yolk

2 tablespoons white wine vinegar

3 tablespoons extra virgin olive oil

5 cups chopped romaine lettuce

Finely grated Parmigiano-Reggiano, for garnish

BAKING OPTIONS

With a pizza stone. Preheat the stone in the oven at 400°F for 30 to 45 minutes; or preheat the stone on a gas grill at medium, indirect heat (about 400°F) for 30 to 45 minutes; or build an indirect, medium-heat coal bed in a charcoal grill and preheat the stone for the same amount of time.

With a pizza tray or baking sheet. Preheat the oven to 400°F, a gas grill to indirect, medium heat (about 400°F), or build an indirect, medium-heat coal bed around the perimeter of a charcoal grill.

CRUST OPTIONS

Fresh dough on a pizza stone. Dust a pizza peel lightly with flour, then place the dough at its center. Dimple it into a large circle with your fingertips, then pick it up and shape it by holding its edge and rotating it slowly, stretching the edge a little as you do so, until it's a circle about 14 inches in diameter. Set it floured side down on the peel.

Fresh dough on a pizza tray or a baking sheet. Use a little olive oil on a paper towel to grease a pizza tray or a large baking sheet. Lay the dough on the tray or baking sheet; dimple the dough with your fingertips until it looks like a flattened circle. Then pull and press it until it's a 14-inch circle on the tray or an irregular rectangle, perhaps 12 × 7 inches, on the baking sheet.

A prebaked crust. Place it on a pizza peel if you're also using a pizza stone—or place the prebaked crust right on a large baking sheet.

1. Spray a large skillet with nonstick spray, set it over medium heat, add the chicken breasts, and cook until browned and cooked through, about 12 minutes, turning occasionally. Alternatively, spray the breasts themselves with nonstick spray and grill them on the grill rack directly over the heat until cooked through, turning occasionally, about 12 minutes. Set aside for 5 minutes, then slice into thin strips.

2. Spread the honey mustard evenly over the crust, leaving a ½-inch border at the edge. Top the honey mustard with the shredded mozzarella, then place the sliced chicken breasts and chopped bell pepper over the cheese.

3. Slip the crust from the peel to the heated stone or place the pie on the pizza tray or the baking sheet either in the oven or on the grill over the unheated section of the grate. Bake or grill with the lid closed until the cheese has melted and the crust is lightly browned, about 18 minutes.

4. Slip the peel back under the crust to remove it from the very hot stone—or transfer the pie on the tray or baking sheet to a wire rack. In either case, cool the crust for 5 minutes.

5. Meanwhile, use a fork to mash the garlic, anchovies, salt, and pepper in the bottom of a large bowl until pastelike and fairly smooth. Whisk in the egg yolk and vinegar, then whisk in the olive oil in a slow, steady stream until creamy. Add the chopped romaine and toss well to coat.

6. Slip the pizza off the peel, the tray, or the baking sheet, placing it directly on a large cutting board. Mound the dressed lettuce over the pizza. If desired, sprinkle on the grated Parmigiano-Reggiano before slicing into wedges to serve.

Steak and Arugula Pizza

In the summer, we love a grilled steak and arugula salad with crunchy bread—so we decided we'd combine them all for this nontraditional pie. You'll need to blind-bake the crust and also to sear the steak, either on the grill or in a grill pan.

MAKES 1 PIZZA

Either all-purpose flour for the pizza peel or nonstick spray for the pizza tray or the baking sheet

One recipe homemade dough, preferably the Classic Pizza Dough (page 23); or 1 pound purchased fresh dough or frozen dough, thawed; or one 12- to 14-inch store-bought, prebaked plain pizza crust

3 tablespoons olive oil

½ teaspoon freshly ground black pepper

8 ounces (½ pound) sirloin steak, trimmed

6 tablespoons Pizza Pesto (page 40) or purchased, low-oil pesto

½ cup finely chopped sun-dried tomatoes packed in oil

3 ounces Asiago, finely grated

1 tablespoon balsamic vinegar

½ teaspoon salt

4 cups packed chopped arugula

BAKING OPTIONS

With a pizza stone. Preheat the stone in the oven at 400°F for 30 to 45 minutes; or preheat the stone on a gas grill at medium, indirect heat (about 400°F) for 30 to 45 minutes; or build an indirect, medium-heat coal bed in a charcoal grill and preheat the stone for the same amount of time.

With a pizza tray or a large baking sheet. Preheat the oven to 400°F, a gas grill to indirect, medium heat (about 400°F), or build an indirect, medium-heat coal bed around the perimeter of a charcoal grill.

CRUST OPTIONS

Fresh dough on a pizza stone. Dust a pizza peel with flour. Add the dough and form it into a large circle by dimpling it with your fingertips. Pick it up and shape it with your hands, holding its edge, slowly turning the dough and stretching its edge gently all the while until the circle is about 14 inches in diameter. Set the dough floured side down on the peel.

Fresh dough on a pizza tray or a large baking sheet. Grease the tray or baking sheet with nonstick spray. Lay the dough at the center; dimple the dough into a flat, thick circle with your fingertips—then pull and press it until it forms a circle about 14 inches in diameter on the tray or an irregular rectangle, perhaps 12 × 7 inches, on the baking sheet.

A prebaked crust. Place it on a floured pizza peel if you're also using a pizza stone—or place the prebaked crust on a pizza tray or a large baking sheet.

1. If you're working with a purchased, prebaked crust, skip this step. If you're working with shaped, fresh dough, slide it from the peel onto the very hot stone or place it on its tray or baking sheet either in the oven or over the unheated portion of the grill grate. Bake or grill with the lid closed until lightly browned, about 12 minutes. Air bubbles may arise over the crust while it bakes; pop these with a fork to assure an even crust. Slide the peel back under the crust to get it off the stone or transfer the crust on the tray or baking sheet to a wire rack.

2. While the crust cools slightly, rub 1 tablespoon of the olive oil and the pepper into the sirloin. Either heat a grill pan over medium-high heat, then add the steak—or place the steak on the grill grate directly over the heat. Cook just until seared on the outside but still quite red and raw in the middle, 1 to 2 minutes per side. Transfer to a cutting board.

3. Spread the pesto evenly over the crust, leaving a ½-inch border at its edge. Top with the sun-dried tomatoes.

4. Run your fingers across the steak to see which way the fibers are running. Slice the steak into thin strips at a 90-degree angle from the direction of these fibers. Lay these strips over the pizza, then top with the grated Asiago.

5. Once again, slide the pizza from the peel to the heated stone or place the pie on its tray or baking sheet with the now-topped pizza back in the oven or over the unheated section of the grill grate. Bake or grill with the lid closed until the cheese has melted and the steak is sizzling, about 10 minutes. Slide the peel back under the pizza on the hot stone to remove it and set it aside—or transfer the pie on its tray or baking sheet to a wire rack.

6. Whisk the vinegar, salt, and the remaining 2 tablespoons olive oil in a large bowl. Add the arugula and toss to coat. Mound on top of the pizza, then slice into wedges to serve.

SEVENTEEN
INTERNATIONAL
PIZZAS

Pizza is not just Italian fare. In fact, some culinary histories dare to suggest the whole thing got started in Germany, not Italy. Be that as it may, pizzas or their imitators now exist the world over. There are pies from various regions like the Alsatian Tarte Flambé (page 139) or the Lamejun Pizza from Armenia (page 142). We've reinterpreted these as American pies but tried to keep the flavors in line with the originals. That said, we haven't gone so far as to count quesadillas as pizzas; instead, we've adhered to a more standard model here.

Even so, there are some rather whimsical reinterpretations of international dishes—like the Raclette Pizza (page 169) or the Lamb Tagine Pizza (page 160). Basically, we've taken the flavors of the dish in question and transferred them to a pie with some modifications to compensate for the short cooking time a pizza gets over the heat.

Every pizza in this section is a main-course pie, perfect for lunch or dinner. All in all, this is an international set of flavors, none hewing to authenticity but all well beyond the pepperoni standard.

Alsatian Tarte Flambé

As with most regional dishes, there are hundreds of variations; all have their defenders. But we'll say it up front: this is an American-style pie modeled after the classic Alsatian *tarte* of onions, bacon, and cream.

MAKES 1 PIZZA

Either all-purpose flour for the pizza peel or nonstick spray for the pizza tray or the baking sheet

One recipe homemade dough, preferably the Classic Pizza Dough (page 23); or 1 pound purchased fresh dough or frozen dough, thawed; or one 12- to 14-inch store-bought, prebaked plain pizza crust

6 ounces bacon strips

1 medium yellow onion, halved through the stem, then thinly sliced

¼ cup dry white wine or dry vermouth

1 cup crème fraîche

¼ teaspoon grated or ground nutmeg

¼ teaspoon freshly ground black pepper (see Note)

BAKING OPTIONS

With a pizza stone. Preheat the stone in the oven at 450°F for 30 to 45 minutes; or preheat the stone on a gas grill at medium, indirect heat (about 450°F) for 30 to 45 minutes; or build an indirect, medium-heat coal bed in a charcoal grill and preheat the stone for the same amount of time.

With a pizza tray or a large baking sheet. Preheat the oven to 450°F, a gas grill to indirect, medium heat (about 450°F), or build an indirect, medium-heat fire around the perimeter of a charcoal grill.

CRUST OPTIONS

Fresh pizza dough on a pizza stone. Dust a pizza peel lightly with flour. Add the dough and form it into a large circle by dimpling it with your fingertips. Pick up the dough and rotate it by its edge to shape it into a circle about 14 inches in diameter. Set it floured side down onto the peel.

Fresh dough on a pizza tray or a large baking sheet. Grease the tray or baking sheet lightly with nonstick spray. Lay the dough on the tray or baking sheet and dimple it with your fingertips—then pull and press the dough until it forms a circle about 14 inches in diameter on the tray or an irregular rectangle, about 12 inches long and 7 inches wide, on the baking sheet.

A prebaked crust. Place it on a pizza peel if you're also using a pizza stone—or place the prebaked crust right on a pizza tray or large baking sheet.

1. Heat a large skillet over medium heat. Add the bacon strips and cook until somewhat browned but still limp, 3 to 4 minutes. (They will cook more thoroughly on top of the pie.) Transfer to a plate.

2. Add the onions to the bacon fat in the skillet and cook, stirring occasionally, until wilted, soft, and quite fragrant, about 8 minutes.

3. Pour in the wine and raise the heat to medium-high. As the wine simmers, scrape up any browned bits on the skillet's bottom. Continue cooking at a full simmer until the liquid in the skillet is a thick glaze over the onions, about 4 minutes.

4. Spread the crème fraîche over the prepared crust, keeping a ½-inch border at the edge. Chop the bacon and sprinkle it over the pie.

5. Use a rubber spatula to spoon and spread the softened onions and their glaze over the pizza, again keeping that border intact. Sprinkle with the nutmeg and pepper. Slide the pizza from its peel onto the heated stone, taking care not to dislodge the toppings—or place the pizza on the pizza tray or the baking sheet either in the oven or on the section of the grill grate that's not right over the heat source.

6. Bake or grill with the lid closed until the crust is golden brown and somewhat firm to the touch, 16 to 18 minutes. Should any air bubbles arise on fresh dough, particularly after about 10 minutes, prick them with a fork to ensure an even crust. Slip the peel back under the pizza and take it off the hot stone—or transfer the pizza on the pizza tray or baking sheet to a wire rack. In either case, set aside to cool for 5 minutes before slicing and serving.

NOTE: There's no salt in the topping because the bacon is salty. Pass extra salt on the side for those who'd like more. Also consider passing some red pepper flakes with the cooled wedges

Lamejun Pizza

Originally an Armenian specialty, this thick mixture of ground lamb, tomatoes, and spices is baked on a thin crust, sort of like tortillas. The pies are often stacked one on top of the other on the table. Here, that traditional mixture is put on top of an American pizza crust.

MAKES 1 PIZZA

All-purpose flour for the pizza peel or olive oil for the pizza tray or the baking sheet

One recipe homemade dough, preferably the Classic Pizza Dough (page 23) or the Cracker Pizza Dough (page 35); or 1 pound purchased fresh dough or frozen dough, thawed; or one 12- to 14-inch store-bought, prebaked plain pizza crust

2 tablespoons olive oil

1 medium red onion, chopped

8 ounces (½ pound) ground lamb

12 cherry tomatoes, chopped

2 tablespoons minced parsley leaves or 1 tablespoon dried parsley

1 teaspoon ground cinnamon

½ teaspoon salt

½ teaspoon freshly ground black pepper

1 tablespoon pomegranate molasses (see Note)

1 tablespoon pine nuts

BAKING OPTIONS

With a pizza stone. Preheat the stone in the oven at 450°F for 30 to 45 minutes; or preheat the stone on a gas grill at medium, indirect heat (about 450°F) for 30 to 45 minutes; or build an indirect, medium-heat coal bed in a charcoal grill and preheat the stone for the same amount of time.

With a pizza tray or a large baking sheet. Preheat the oven to 450°F, a gas grill to indirect, medium heat (about 450°F), or build an indirect, medium-heat coal bed around the perimeter of a charcoal grill.

CRUST OPTIONS

Fresh dough on a pizza stone. Start out by dusting a pizza peel with flour, then set the dough at its center. Form the dough into a large circle by dimpling it with your fingertips. Pick it up and shape it by holding its edge in both hands and slowly rotating the dough, stretching it all the while, until it's a circle about 14 inches in diameter. Set it floured side down on the peel. If using Cracker Pizza Dough, you cannot pick it up because the dough itself is too fragile; follow the shaping instructions on page 35.

Fresh dough on a pizza tray or a baking sheet. Grease the tray or baking sheet with some olive oil dabbed on a paper towel. Lay the dough on the tray or baking sheet; dimple the dough with your fingertips—then pull and press the dough until it forms a 14-inch circle on the tray or a 12×7-inch irregular rectangle on the baking sheet.

A prebaked crust. Place it on a pizza peel if you're also using a pizza stone—or place the prebaked crust on a pizza tray or a large baking sheet.

1. Heat a large skillet over medium heat. Swirl in the olive oil, then add the onion. Cook, stirring often, until softened, about 3 minutes.

2. Crumble in the ground lamb; cook, stirring often, until lightly browned, about 8 minutes.

3. Stir in the chopped cherry tomatoes, parsley, cinnamon, salt, and pepper. Continue cooking until the tomatoes break down and make a somewhat thickened sauce, about 5 minutes. Cool at room temperature for 20 minutes.

4. Spread the lamb mixture over the prepared crust, making sure you leave a ½-inch border at the edge.

5. Drizzle with the pomegranate molasses and top with the pine nuts. Taking care not to jostle the toppings, gently slip the pizza from the peel to the hot stone—or place the pie on its tray or baking sheet either in the oven or on top of the section of the grill grate that's not directly over the heat source or coals.

6. Bake or grill with the lid closed until the crust is golden at its edge and perhaps even a little darkened on its underside, 18 to 20 minutes. If you're working with homemade or purchased fresh dough, check it occasionally to prick any air bubbles that may arise on its surface. Slip the peel back under the pie to take it off the stone, again taking care to keep that topping in place—or transfer the pie on the tray or the baking sheet to a wire rack. Set aside to cool for 5 minutes before slicing and serving.

NOTE: Pomegranate molasses is a thick, dark syrup made from an especially tart variety of pomegranate; the juice is boiled until it's a thick syrup, sort of like molasses but more sour and pungent. It's a staple in Middle Eastern cooking and can be found in almost all Asian, Middle Eastern, and Indian markets, and even some supermarkets.

Thai Chicken Pizza

Here's an internationally inspired pie that's become quite popular at some national pizza chains. Make a double batch of this spicy peanut sauce, store it in the refrigerator for a few days, and use it as dip for cut-up vegetables or an excellent topping for pasta, particularly Japanese udon noodles.

MAKES 1 PIZZA

Either all-purpose flour to dust the pizza peel or nonstick spray to grease the pizza tray or a large baking sheet

One recipe homemade dough, preferably the Semolina Pizza Dough (page 29); or 1 pound purchased fresh dough or frozen dough, thawed; or one 12- to 14-inch store-bought, prebaked plain pizza crust

2 tablespoons creamy peanut butter

1 tablespoon Asian oyster sauce

2 teaspoons toasted sesame oil

1 teaspoon regular or reduced-sodium soy sauce

1 teaspoon rice vinegar

1 teaspoon sugar

1 teaspoon minced peeled fresh ginger

½ teaspoon Asian red chile sauce or sambal oelek

4 ounces mozzarella, Swiss, or Emmental, shredded

1 cup chopped, cooked chicken meat (see Note)

6 medium scallions, thinly sliced

3 tablespoons chopped roasted peanuts

BAKING OPTIONS

With a pizza stone. Preheat the stone in the oven at 450°F for 30 to 45 minutes; or preheat the stone on a gas grill at medium, indirect heat (about 450°F) for 30 to 45 minutes; or build an indirect, medium-heat coal bed in a charcoal grill and preheat the stone for the same amount of time.

With a pizza tray or a large baking sheet. Preheat the oven to 450°F, a gas grill to indirect, medium heat (about 450°F), or build an indirect, medium-heat coal bed around the perimeter of a charcoal grill.

CRUST OPTIONS

Fresh dough on a pizza stone. Dust a pizza peel with flour. Add the dough and form it into a large circle by dimpling it with your fingertips. Pick it up and shape the dough by holding its edge in both hands and slowly rotating it, stretching the edge all the while, until it's a circle about 14 inches in diameter. Set it floured side down on the peel.

Fresh dough on a pizza tray or a large baking sheet. Grease the tray or baking sheet with nonstick spray. Lay the dough at the center of either; dimple the dough with your fingertips into a flat, thick circle—then pull and press the dough until it forms a 14-inch circle on the tray or a 12 × 7-inch somewhat irregular rectangle on the baking sheet.

A prebaked crust. Place it on a pizza peel if you're also using a pizza stone—or place the prebaked crust right on a pizza tray or a large baking sheet.

1. Place the peanut butter, oyster sauce, sesame oil, soy sauce, rice vinegar, sugar, ginger, and chile sauce in a food processor or a blender. Process or blend until smooth, scraping down the inside of the bowl or canister as necessary. Spread the mixture evenly over the prepared crust, leaving a ½-inch border at the edge.

2. Sprinkle the shredded cheese over the sauce, then top with the chopped chicken, scallions, and peanuts. Taking care not to dislodge the toppings, slide the pizza from the peel to the preheated stone or place the tray or baking pan holding the pie either in the oven or over the section of the grill grate that's not directly over the heat or coals.

3. Bake or grill with the lid closed until the crust is golden brown and somewhat firm, 14 to 16 minutes. Check fresh dough during the first 10 minutes so you can use a fork to prick any air bubbles that may arise, particularly at the edge. Slide the peel back under the pizza or transfer the pie on its tray or baking sheet to a wire rack. Set aside to cool for 5 minutes before slicing. To make sure the crust stays crunchy, consider transferring the still-hot pie from the peel, tray, or baking sheet right to the wire rack after a minute or so.

NOTE: To get this amount of cooked chicken meat, either buy a rotisserie chicken, skin it, and take the meat off the bones; or sauté a couple of boneless skinless chicken breasts with a little oil in a skillet set over medium heat, turning occasionally, until cooked through, until an instant-read meat thermometer inserted into one of the breasts registers 165°F.

Eggplant Parmesan Pizza

Here's a no-fry version of the Italian-American classic—and on a pizza, to boot! You'll need to bake or grill the eggplant before you put it on top of the pie. Even on the grill, use a baking sheet to allow the eggplant slices to dry evenly and to prevent a mess. Excess moisture from those slices can lead to a soggy crust. The temperature for the grill or oven is at first slightly lower here so you can grill or bake the eggplant slices safely with no fear of their scorching.

MAKES 1 PIZZA

Yellow cornmeal for dusting the pizza peel or olive oil for greasing the pizza tray or the baking sheet

One recipe homemade dough, preferably the Olive Oil Pizza Dough (page 27); or 1 pound purchased fresh dough or frozen dough, thawed; or one 12- to 14-inch store-bought, prebaked plain pizza crust

1 small eggplant, cut into ¼-inch-thick slices (do not peel)

2 tablespoons olive oil

½ teaspoon salt

¼ cup Classic Pizza Sauce (page 38), No-Cook Pizza Sauce (page 39), or jarred plain pizza sauce

3 ounces mozzarella, shredded

2 ounces chopped prosciutto, optional

2½ ounces Parmigiano-Reggiano, shaved into thin strips

Up to ½ teaspoon red pepper flakes

Up to ½ teaspoon grated nutmeg, ground mace, or ground cinnamon

BAKING OPTIONS

With a pizza stone. Preheat the stone in the oven at 400°F for 30 to 45 minutes; or preheat the stone on a gas grill at medium, indirect heat (about 400°F) for 30

to 45 minutes; or build an indirect, medium-heat coal bed in a charcoal grill and preheat the stone for the same amount of time.

With a pizza tray or a large baking sheet. Preheat the oven to 400°F, a gas grill to indirect, medium heat (about 400°F), or build an indirect, medium-heat fire around the perimeter of a charcoal grill.

CRUST OPTIONS

Fresh dough on a pizza stone. Start by lightly dusting a pizza peel with cornmeal. Add the dough and form it into a large circle by dimpling it with your fingertips. Pick up the dough's edge and shape the crust by slowly turning it until it's about 14 inches in diameter. Set the dough cornmeal side down on the peel.

Fresh dough on a pizza tray or a large baking sheet. Grease the tray or baking sheet lightly with olive oil. Lay the dough on either and dimple the dough with your fingertips—then pull and press it until it forms a circle about 14 inches in diameter on the tray or an irregular rectangle, about 12 inches long and 7 inches wide, on the baking sheet.

A prebaked crust. Place it on a cornmeal-dusted pizza peel if you're also using a pizza stone—or place the prebaked crust on a pizza tray or a large baking sheet.

1. Lay the eggplant slices on a large baking sheet; brush them with olive oil and sprinkle with salt.

2. Bake or grill the eggplant on the baking sheet until tender but still a little firm, about 15 minutes. Set aside and increase the oven or grill temperature to 450°F (if using a charcoal grill, add some fresh charcoal briquets now).

3. Spread the pizza sauce over the prepared dough, taking care to leave a ½-inch border at the edge. Top with the shredded mozzarella.

4. Lay the eggplant slices over the pie, overlapping as necessary—then tuck in the prosciutto, if desired. Top with the shaved Parmigiano-Reggiano slices, then sprinkle with the red pepper flakes and ground spice, as desired. Slide the pie from the peel to the hot stone or transfer the pie on its pizza tray or baking sheet either to the oven or to the part of the grill grate that's not directly over the heat source.

5. Bake or grill with the lid closed until the cheese has melted and started to brown, until the crust is golden and somewhat firm to the touch, 16 to 18 minutes. Slip the peel back under the pizza to take it off the hot stone—or transfer the pie on the tray or the baking sheet to a wire rack. Set aside to cool for 5 minutes before slicing.

BLT Pizza (page 125)

 White Clam Pizza (page 61)

Lamejun Pizza (page 142)

Cherry Tomato and Pancetta Pizza (page 89)

Mushroom Lovers' Deep-Dish Pizza (page 265)

Four Seasons Pizza (page 55)

Winter Squash, Onion, and Pine Nut Pizza (page 83)

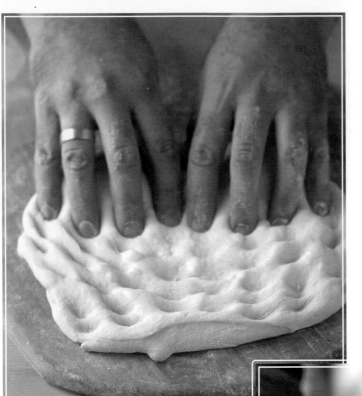

Massaging the dough

Stretching the dough

Puttanesca Pizza

Puttanesca is a spicy sauce made up of Italian pantry staples—olives, anchovies, capers, garlic, and the like—and a great topping for a pie!

MAKES 1 PIZZA

Yellow cornmeal for dusting a pizza peel or olive oil for greasing a pizza tray or a large baking sheet

One recipe homemade dough, preferably the Olive Oil Pizza Dough (page 27); or 1 pound purchased fresh dough or frozen dough, thawed; or one 12- to 14-inch store-bought, prebaked plain pizza crust

4 ounces (¼ pound) Parmigiano-Reggiano, shaved into thin strips

12 ounces (¾ pound) plum or Roma tomatoes, chopped (about 1½ cups)

1 jarred whole pimiento or roasted red pepper, chopped

2 tinned anchovy fillets, minced

2 garlic cloves, minced

¼ cup chopped pitted black olives

¼ cup diced red onion

1 tablespoon capers, drained, rinsed, and minced

1 teaspoon minced rosemary leaves or ½ teaspoon dried rosemary, crumbled

1 teaspoon minced oregano leaves or ½ teaspoon dried oregano

Up to ½ teaspoon red pepper flakes

¼ teaspoon salt

BAKING OPTIONS

With a pizza stone. Preheat the stone in the oven at 450°F for 30 to 45 minutes; or preheat the stone on a gas grill at medium, indirect heat (about 450°F) for 30 to 45 minutes; or build an indirect, medium-heat coal bed in a charcoal grill and preheat the stone for the same amount of time.

With a pizza tray or a large baking sheet. Preheat the oven to 450°F, a gas grill to indirect, medium heat (about 450°F), or build an indirect, medium-heat coal bed around the perimeter of a charcoal grill.

CRUST OPTIONS

Fresh dough on a pizza stone. Dust a pizza peel lightly with cornmeal. Add the dough and form it into a large circle by dimpling it with your fingertips. Pick it up and shape it with your hands, holding its edge, slowly turning and stretching the dough until it's about 14 inches in diameter. Set it cornmeal side down on the peel.

Fresh dough on a pizza tray or a large baking sheet. Grease the tray or baking sheet with a little olive oil dabbed on a paper towel. Lay the dough on the tray or baking sheet; dimple the dough with your fingertips until it's a flattened, thick circle—then pull and press it until it forms a 14-inch circle on the tray or an irregular 12 × 7-inch rectangle on the baking sheet.

A prebaked crust. Place it on a floured pizza peel if you're also using a pizza stone—or place the prebaked crust on a pizza tray or a large baking sheet.

1. Lay three-quarters of the strips of shaved Parmigiano-Reggiano over the prepared crust, taking care to leave a ½-inch border at the edge.

2. Mix the tomatoes, pimiento, anchovies, garlic, olives, onion, capers, rosemary, oregano, red pepper flakes to taste, and the salt in a large bowl. Spread this mixture evenly over the cheese on the crust, taking care not to dislodge the strips.

3. Slip the pizza from the peel to the hot stone or place the pizza on the tray or the baking sheet either in the oven or over the unheated portion of the grill grate. Bake or grill with the lid closed until the crust is firm and golden at its edge, 16 to 18 minutes. Fresh doughs may develop air bubbles, which should be popped with a fork to produce an even crust.

4. Lay the remaining pieces of shaved Parmigiano-Reggiano over the hot pie.

5. Slide the peel back under the pizza, taking care not to dislodge the toppings and set the pizza aside on the peel to cool for 5 minutes—or transfer the pizza on the tray or baking sheet to a wire rack where it, too, can cool for 5 minutes before slicing and serving. To make sure the crust stays crisp, consider transferring the pie from the peel, tray, or baking sheet directly to the wire rack after a minute or so before cooling for the remaining 3 or 4 minutes.

Melanzane Pizza

Pasta Melanzane is a traditional dish of eggplant in a rich tomato sauce served over ziti or other macaroni Here, that eggplant stew is put over pizza sauce on a traditional crust.

MAKES 1 PIZZA

Yellow cornmeal for dusting a pizza peel or olive oil for greasing a pizza tray or a large baking sheet

One recipe homemade dough, preferably the Olive Oil Pizza Dough (page 27); or 1 pound purchased fresh dough or frozen dough, thawed; or one 12- to 14-inch store-bought, prebaked plain pizza crust

One 12-ounce (¾-pound) eggplant, stemmed but not peeled

¼ cup olive oil

4 garlic cloves, minced

2 teaspoons minced oregano leaves or 1 teaspoon dried oregano

½ teaspoon salt

½ teaspoon freshly ground black pepper

1 cup dry white wine or dry vermouth

½ cup Classic Pizza Sauce (page 38), No-Cook Pizza Sauce (page 39), or jarred plain pizza sauce

1 cup regular, low-fat, or fat-free ricotta, at room temperature

4 ounces mozzarella, shredded

1 ounce Parmigiano-Reggiano, Grana Padano, or Pecorino, finely grated

BAKING OPTIONS

With a pizza stone. Preheat the stone in the oven at 450°F for 30 to 45 minutes; or preheat the stone on a gas grill at medium, indirect heat (about 450°F) for 30 to 45 minutes; or build an indirect, medium-heat coal bed in a charcoal grill and preheat the stone for the same amount of time.

With a pizza tray or a large baking sheet. Preheat the oven to 450°F, a gas grill to indirect, medium heat (about 450°F), or build an indirect, medium-heat coal bed around the perimeter of a charcoal grill.

CRUST OPTIONS

Fresh dough on a pizza stone. Dust a pizza peel with cornmeal; set the dough in its center. Dimple the dough into a large, flattened circle with your fingertips, then pick it up and pull and stretch it by its edge until it's about 14 inches in diameter. Set it cornmeal side down on the peel.

Fresh dough on a pizza tray or a large baking sheet. Grease either with a little olive oil. Lay the dough at the center and dimple it with your fingertips—then pull and press the dough until it forms a 14-inch circle on the tray or an irregular 12 × 7-inch rectangle on the baking sheet.

A prebaked crust. Place it on a pizza peel if you're also using a pizza stone—or place the prebaked crust right on the pizza tray or a large baking sheet.

1. Cut the eggplant into ½-inch rounds, then cut these into ½-inch strips.

2. Heat a large skillet over medium heat, pour in the olive oil, and add the eggplant strips. Cook, stirring often, for 5 minutes.

3. Stir in the garlic, oregano, salt, and pepper. Continue cooking, stirring all the while, for 1 minute.

4. Pour in ½ cup of the wine or vermouth, raise the heat to medium-high, and cook, stirring constantly, until it evaporates, about 3 minutes.

5. Pour in the remaining ½ cup wine or vermouth and again cook, stirring constantly, until it evaporates. Remove the skillet from the heat and cool for 10 minutes.

6. Spread the pizza sauce evenly over the prepared crust, taking care to leave a ½-inch border at its perimeter. Use a rubber spatula to gently spread the ricotta over the sauce. Top with the eggplant mixture in the skillet.

7. Mix the shredded mozzarella and the finely grated cheese in a medium bowl until well combined, then sprinkle over the pie. Slide it from the peel to the preheated stone or place the pie on the pizza tray or the baking sheet either in the oven or on the portion of the grill's grate that's not directly over the heat source.

8. Bake or grill with the lid closed until the cheese has melted and the crust is golden brown as well as somewhat firm, 16 to 18 minutes. Air bubbles may inflate along the edge of fresh dough; pop them with a fork to assure an even crust. Slide the peel back under the pizza to remove it from the very hot stone or transfer the pie on its tray or baking sheet with its pie to a wire rack. Set aside to cool for 5 minutes before slicing. To make sure the crust stays crisp, transfer the pie from the peel, tray, or baking sheet right to the wire rack after a minute or two.

Enchilada Pizza

No tortillas required—but in this Tex-Mex take on pizza, a classic enchilada sauce is used on the pie. The recipe yields twice as much sauce as you need, but you can freeze the other half for the next pie—or just make half a recipe for one pie. Look for supple, brightly colored dried chiles without any rot or discoloration at their stems.

MAKES 1 PIZZA (AND 1½ CUPS ENCHILADA SAUCE)

Either yellow cornmeal for the pizza peel or nonstick spray for the pizza tray or the baking sheet

One recipe homemade dough, preferably the Classic Pizza Dough (page 23); or 1 pound purchased fresh dough or frozen dough, thawed; or one 12- to 14-inch store-bought, prebaked plain pizza crust

1 tablespoon canola oil

1 small yellow onion, chopped (about ¾ cup)

2 garlic cloves, minced

6 dried New Mexican red chiles, stemmed, seeded, and deveined—or a mixture of any 6 dried chiles, provided the hotter chiles like chipotles and habaneros are kept to a minimum

2 teaspoons minced oregano leaves or 1 teaspoon dried oregano

½ teaspoon salt

1½ cups reduced-sodium fat-free chicken broth

4 ounces Cheddar, shredded

2 cups chopped, skinned, and deboned rotisserie chicken meat or 12 ounces chopped cooked boneless skinless chicken breasts (see page 147 for instructions on how to cook them)

1 cup canned pinto beans, drained and rinsed

2 ounces queso blanco or shredded Monterey Jack

BAKING OPTIONS

With a pizza stone. Position the rack in the middle of the oven and preheat the stone in the oven at 450°F for 30 to 45 minutes; or preheat the stone on a gas grill at medium, indirect heat (about 450°F) for 30 to 45 minutes; or build an indirect, medium-heat coal bed in a charcoal grill and then preheat the stone for the same amount of time.

With a pizza tray or a baking sheet. Preheat the oven to 450°F, a gas grill to indirect, medium heat (about 450°F), or build an indirect, medium-heat coal bed around the perimeter of a charcoal grill.

CRUST OPTIONS

Fresh dough on a pizza stone. Start out by dusting a pizza peel with cornmeal. Set the dough in the center of the peel and dimple the dough with your fingertips until it's a thick, flattened circle. Pick it up and shape it by holding its edge and slowly turning it, stretching it all the while at the edge, until it's about 14 inches in diameter. Set it back on the peel floured side down.

Fresh dough on a pizza tray or a large baking sheet. Grease one or the other with nonstick spray. Lay the dough on the tray or baking sheet; dimple it with your fingertips—then pull and press it until it forms a 14-inch circle on the tray or an irregular 12 × 7-inch rectangle on the baking sheet.

A prebaked crust. Place it on a cornmeal-dusted pizza peel if you're also using a pizza stone—or place the prebaked crust on a pizza tray or a large baking sheet.

1. Heat the oil in a medium saucepan over medium heat. Add the onion and garlic; cook until softened, stirring occasionally, about 3 minutes.

2. Add the chiles, oregano, and salt; cook, stirring constantly, for 30 seconds. Pour in the broth and bring to a simmer. Cover, reduce the heat to low, and simmer slowly for 20 minutes.

3. Pour the entire contents of the pan into a large blender. Cover but remove the small venting cap in the center of the blender lid. Cover the hole loosely with several folded paper towels or a clean kitchen towel, then blend until smooth. Cool at room temperature for 20 minutes.

4. Spread about ¾ cup of the enchilada sauce over the crust, maintaining a ½-inch border at the crust's edge. (Store the remainder of the sauce in a sealed container in the refrigerator for up to 3 days or in the freezer for up to 3 months.)

5. Sprinkle the shredded Cheddar over the sauce, preserving the border at the edge. Top with the cooked chicken and pinto beans. Crumble the queso blanco or sprinkle the Monterey Jack evenly over the toppings.

6. Slip the pie from the peel onto the heated stone or place the pie on its pizza tray or the baking sheet in the oven or over the unheated section of the grill. Bake or grill with the lid closed until the cheese has melted and the crust is lightly browned, about 18 minutes. Slip the peel back under the crust to remove it from the stone and set aside to cool for 5 minutes before slicing—or transfer the pie on the tray or baking sheet to a wire rack and cool for the same amount of time before slicing. In either case, consider removing the pie from the peel, tray, or baking sheet after a minute or two and setting it directly on the wire rack so that the crust isn't in contact with a solid surface while it cools.

Lamb Tagine Pizza

A tagine is a Moroccan stew made with fragrant, dried spices and pre-served lemons. Look for these ingredients in the specialty food aisle of many supermarkets or in Middle Eastern and East Indian culinary suppliers on the Web. The lemons are quite salty, so rinse them before using them.

MAKES 1 PIZZA

Either all-purpose flour to dust the pizza peel or nonstick spray to grease the pizza tray or a large baking sheet

One recipe homemade dough, preferably the Whole Wheat Pizza Dough (page 25); or 1 pound purchased fresh dough or frozen dough, thawed; or one 12- to 14-inch store-bought, prebaked plain pizza crust

8 ounces (½ pound) ground lamb

2 teaspoons ground coriander

1 teaspoon ground cinnamon

1 teaspoon ground cumin

1 teaspoon ground ginger

1 teaspoon freshly ground black pepper

¼ teaspoon saffron

1 tablespoon canola oil

⅔ cup canned chickpeas, drained and rinsed

1 preserved lemon, halved, insides discarded, the rind finely chopped

⅓ cup fat-free reduced-sodium chicken broth

2 teaspoons honey

4 ounces (¼ pound) mozzarella, shredded

BAKING OPTIONS

With a pizza stone. Preheat the stone in the oven at 450°F for 30 to 45 minutes; or preheat the stone on a gas grill at medium, indirect heat (about 450°F) for 30

to 45 minutes; or build an indirect, medium-heat coal bed in a charcoal grill and preheat the stone for the same amount of time.

With a pizza tray or a baking sheet. Preheat the oven to 450°F, a gas grill to indirect, medium heat (about 450°F), or build an indirect, medium-heat coal bed around the perimeter of a charcoal grill.

CRUST OPTIONS

Fresh dough on a pizza stone. Dust a pizza peel with flour. Add the dough and form it into a large circle by dimpling it with your fingertips. Pick it up by its edge and shape it by letting gravity pull it down as you slowly rotate it, stretching the dough at its edge all the while, until it's a circle about 14 inches in diameter. Set the dough floured side down on the peel.

Fresh dough on a pizza tray or a large baking sheet. Grease the tray or baking sheet with nonstick spray. Lay the dough at the center of either; dimple the dough with your fingertips—then pull and press it until it forms a 14-inch circle on the tray or an irregular rectangle, about 12 × 7 inches, on the baking sheet.

A prebaked crust. Place it on a floured pizza peel if using a pizza stone—or place the prebaked crust on a greased pizza tray or a large baking sheet.

1. Mix the ground lamb with the ground coriander, cinnamon, cumin, ginger, pepper, and saffron in a medium bowl until the meat is well coated and the spices are evenly distributed.

2. Heat a large skillet over medium heat. Swirl in the oil, then add the spiced lamb mixture. Cook, stirring often, until lightly browned, about 6 minutes.

3. Stir in the chickpeas and preserved lemon. Cook, stirring constantly, for 2 minutes.

4. Pour in the broth and continue cooking, stirring often, until it has evaporated from the skillet. Remove from the heat and stir in the honey.

5. Sprinkle the shredded mozzarella evenly over the prepared crust, leaving a ½-inch border at the edge. Top with the ground-lamb mixture. Slide the pie from the peel to the hot stone or place the pie on its tray or baking sheet either in the oven or on the section of the grill grate that's not right over the heat source.

6. Bake or grill with the lid closed until the crust is golden and somewhat firm to the touch, 16 to 18 minutes. Check fresh dough, whether homemade or store-bought, once or twice, particularly after the first 10 minutes, so you can prick any air bubbles that may form. Once the pie is done, slip the peel back under it to take it off the hot stone or transfer the pie on its tray or the baking sheet with its pie to a wire rack. Set aside to cool for 5 minutes before slicing and serving. To ensure a crunchy crust, transfer the hot pie directly to the wire rack after a minute or two.

Tandoori Chicken Pizza

A tandoor is a high-heat oven, often made of clay, used in cooking East Indian food. Tandoori then refers something cooked in that oven, although the term can also refer to a certain yogurt-marinated, spicy main course in East Indian restaurants across North America and Europe.

MAKES 1 PIZZA

Either all-purpose flour for dusting the pizza peel or nonstick spray for greasing the pizza tray or the baking sheet

One recipe homemade dough, preferably the Classic Pizza Dough (page 23); or 1 pound purchased fresh dough or frozen dough, thawed; or one 12- to 14-inch store-bought, prebaked plain pizza crust

10 ounces boneless skinless chicken breasts

½ cup plain regular, low-fat, or fat-free yogurt

2 teaspoons yellow curry powder (see Note)

1 teaspoon ginger juice

½ cup mango chutney, tomato chutney, or any hot or mild chutney

4 ounces (¼ pound) mozzarella, shredded

4 ounces (¼ pound) Monterey Jack, shredded

1 small red onion, very thinly sliced

BAKING OPTIONS

With a pizza stone. Preheat the stone in the oven at 450°F for 30 to 45 minutes; or preheat the stone on a gas grill at medium, indirect heat (about 450°F) for 30 to 45 minutes; or build an indirect, medium-heat coal bed in a charcoal grill and preheat the stone for the same amount of time.

With a pizza tray or a large baking sheet. Preheat the oven to 450°F, a gas grill to indirect, medium heat (about 450°F), or build an indirect, medium-heat fire around the perimeter of a charcoal grill.

CRUST OPTIONS

Fresh dough on a pizza stone. Dust a pizza peel with flour, set the dough at its center, and dimple the dough into a thick, flat circle with your fingertips. Pick it up, hold its edge with both hands, and slowly rotate it, stretching the edge gently as you do so, until the circle is about 14 inches in diameter. Set the dough floured side down on the peel.

Fresh dough on a pizza tray or a large baking sheet. Grease one or the other with nonstick spray. Lay the dough at the center of either; dimple the dough into a thick, flat circle with your fingertips—then pull and press it until it forms a 14-inch circle on the tray or an irregular 12 × 7-inch rectangle on the baking sheet.

A prebaked crust. Place it on a pizza peel if using a pizza stone—or place the prebaked crust on a pizza tray or a large baking sheet.

1. Mix the chicken breasts, yogurt, curry powder, and ginger juice in a large bowl until the meat is evenly coated. Set aside for 10 minutes while preheating the broiler or heat the grill to medium heat.

2. Set the chicken on a large baking sheet to broil 4 to 6 inches from the heat source, or set the chicken directly over the heat on the grill grate. Broil or grill, turning once, until cooked through, and an instant-read meat thermometer inserted into the thickest part of the breasts registers 160°F, about 15 minutes. Transfer to a cutting board and let stand for 5 minutes.

3. Meanwhile, spread the chutney over the prepared dough, leaving a ½-inch border at the edge. Mix the shredded cheeses together in a medium bowl, then sprinkle evenly over the chutney.

4. Slice the breasts into long, thin strips; lay these over the top of the pizza. Lay the red onion slices evenly and decoratively over the pie. Slide the topped pizza from the peel to the hot stone or set the crust on the pizza tray or the baking sheet either in the oven or over the unheated section of the grill grate.

5. Bake or grill with the lid closed until the crust is browned and somewhat firm and the cheese has melted and is starting to bubble, 16 to 18 minutes, popping any air bubbles that may dot the surface of fresh dough. Slip the peel back under the baked pizza to remove it from the stone or transfer the pizza on the tray or the baking sheet to a wire rack. In either case, cool for 5 minutes before slicing and serving.

NOTE: Curry powders are blends of dried spices, with no two alike. To make your own for this pie, try this combination: ½ teaspoon ground coriander, ½ teaspoon ground cumin, ½ teaspoon ground ginger, ¼ teaspoon ground cardamom, ⅛ teaspoon ground cinnamon, and ⅛ teaspoon cayenne.

Curried Vegetable Pizza

While the curry powders are best when made from scratch, you can certainly, as here, doctor the premixed varieties to make them more aromatic, more flavorful. Make sure the vegetables cook until the pan is dry so they don't weigh down the pizza crust with too much liquid.

MAKES 1 PIZZA

Yellow cornmeal to dust the pizza peel or nonstick spray to grease the pizza tray or the large baking sheet

One recipe homemade dough, preferably the Classic Pizza Dough (page 23); or 1 pound purchased fresh dough or frozen dough, thawed; or one 12- to 14-inch store-bought, prebaked plain pizza crust

2 tablespoons vegetable oil

4 medium scallions, thinly sliced

1 tablespoon peeled and minced ginger

1 garlic clove, minced

2 cups diced yellow squash or zucchini

2 cups chopped cauliflower or broccoli florets

2 tablespoons golden raisins

2 teaspoons yellow curry powder plus ½ teaspoon of any two of the following: ground cinnamon, ground mace, dried coriander, dried thyme, ground ginger, and/or ground fenugreek

¼ teaspoon salt

¼ cup dry white wine or dry vermouth

¼ cup mango or other fruit-based chutney

6 ounces mozzarella, shredded

BAKING OPTIONS

With a pizza stone. Preheat the stone in the oven at 450°F for 30 to 45 minutes; or preheat the stone on a gas grill at medium, indirect heat (about 450°F) for 30

to 45 minutes; or build an indirect, medium-heat coal bed in a charcoal grill and preheat the stone for the same amount of time.

With a pizza tray or a baking sheet. Preheat the oven to 450°F, a gas grill to indirect, medium heat (about 450°F), or build an indirect, medium-heat fire around the perimeter of a charcoal grill.

CRUST OPTIONS

Fresh dough on a pizza stone. Dust a pizza peel with cornmeal. Add the dough and form it into a large circle by dimpling it with your fingertips. Pick up the dough and shape it by holding its edge with your hands, slowly turning the dough until it's about 14 inches in diameter. Set it cornmeal side down onto the peel.

Fresh dough on a pizza tray or a large baking sheet. Grease either with nonstick spray. Lay the dough at the center; dimple the dough with your fingertips—then pull and press it until it forms a 14-inch circle on the tray or an irregular 12 × 7-inch rectangle on the baking sheet.

A prebaked crust. Place it on a cornmeal-dusted pizza peel if using a pizza stone—or place the prebaked crust right on a pizza tray or a large baking sheet.

1. Heat the oil in a large skillet set over medium heat. Add the scallions, ginger, and garlic; cook, stirring often, until softened and aromatic, about 1 minute.

2. Add the yellow squash or zucchini, the chopped cauliflower or broccoli, the raisins, curry powder and the other two spices you've chosen, and the salt. Cook, stirring constantly, for 1 minute.

3. Stir in the wine or vermouth; scrape up any browned bits on the skillet's bottom as the liquid comes to a simmer. Cover, reduce the heat to low, and simmer for 5 minutes.

4. Uncover, raise the heat back to medium, and continue simmering until the liquid in the pan has been fully absorbed or evaporated, stirring often, 3 to 5 minutes. Set aside.

5. Spread the chutney over the dough, leaving a ½-inch border at the edge. Sprinkle the shredded mozzarella evenly over the chutney, then top with the vegetable mixture.

6. Slide the pie from the peel to the heated stone or place the pie on the pizza tray or the baking sheet in the oven or on the grill over indirect heat. Bake or grill with the lid closed until the cheese is bubbling and the crust is lightly browned, 16 to 18 minutes. Slip the peel back under the crust to remove it from the stone so it can cool for 5 minutes before slicing—or transfer the pie on the pizza tray or the baking sheet to a wire rack to cool for 5 minutes before serving. To ensure a crisp crust, transfer the pie directly to the wire rack after 1 or 2 minutes so it can cool without resting against another flat surface.

Raclette Pizza

In honor of the famous French Alpine melted-cheese-and-potato dinner, this pizza combines all the ingredients in one pie. Cornichons are small, zippy French gherkins, a good foil to the cheese. There are varieties of raclette made with wine, pepper—even smoked versions. Use only the plain standard for this recipe.

MAKES 1 PIZZA

All-purpose flour to dust the pizza peel or nonstick spray to grease the pizza tray or a large baking sheet

One recipe homemade dough, preferably the Classic Pizza Dough (page 23); or 1 pound purchased fresh dough or frozen dough, thawed; or one 12- to 14-inch store-bought, prebaked plain pizza crust

12 ounces (¾ pound) yellow-fleshed potatoes such as Yukon gold potatoes, peeled and diced

2 tablespoons Dijon mustard

8 ounces (½ pound) raclette, shredded

½ cup chopped cornichons

BAKING OPTIONS

With a pizza stone. Preheat the stone in the oven at 450°F for 30 to 45 minutes; or preheat the stone on a gas grill at medium, indirect heat (about 450°F) for 30 to 45 minutes; or build an indirect, medium-heat coal bed in a charcoal grill and preheat the stone for the same amount of time.

With a pizza tray or a large baking sheet. Preheat the oven to 450°F, a gas grill to indirect, medium heat (about 450°F), or build an indirect, medium-heat coal bed around the perimeter of a charcoal grill.

CRUST OPTIONS

Fresh dough on a pizza stone. Dust a pizza peel lightly with flour. Add the dough and form it into a large circle by dimpling it with your fingertips. Pick it up, hold it by its edge in both hands, and slowly rotate the dough, stretching it gently, until the circle is about 14 inches in diameter. Set the shaped dough floured side down on the peel.

Fresh dough on a pizza tray or a large baking sheet. Grease either with nonstick spray. Lay the dough on the tray or baking sheet; dimple the dough with your fingertips until it's a flattened, thick circle—then pull and press it until it forms a circle about 14 inches in diameter on the tray or a rather irregular rectangle, about 12×7 inches, on the baking sheet.

A prebaked crust. Place it on a floured pizza peel if using a pizza stone—or place the prebaked crust on a pizza tray or a large baking sheet.

1. While the grill or oven heats, bring about 1 inch water to a boil in a saucepan over which or in which is fitted some sort of a vegetable steamer. Place the diced potatoes in the steamer. Cover, reduce the heat to medium, and steam until tender when pierced with a fork, about 6 minutes. Set aside.

2. Spread the mustard evenly over the crust, leaving a $1/2$-inch border at the edge. Top with the shredded raclette, keeping the clean border intact.

3. Spread the hot potatoes over the cheese, then tuck in the chopped cornichons.

4. Slide the pizza from the peel to the very hot stone or place the pie on its tray or baking sheet in the oven or over the section of the grill grate that's not heated. Bake or grill with the lid closed until the cheese is bubbling and just beginning to brown lightly, 16 to 18 minutes. Slip the peel back under the pie—be careful: the cheese-laden pie is delicate and the toppings can slide off—or transfer the pie on its tray or baking sheet to a wire rack. In either case, set aside to cool for 5 minutes before slicing and serving. To ensure a crisp crust, transfer the pie from the peel, tray, or baking sheet right to the wire rack after a minute or so—but again, be careful: the cheese is very hot and the potatoes are slippery until everything sets back up at room temperature.

Ratatouille Pizza

Y ou have to adjust the proportions of this eggplant-and-tomato bistro side dish to make it work on a pizza: the ratatouille must be less watery and more like a sauce. Simmer the ratatouille until the individual vegetables are tender, a little longer than you would if you were making it on its own for a side.

MAKES 1 PIZZA

All-purpose flour for the pizza peel or olive oil for the pizza tray or a large baking sheet

One recipe homemade dough, preferably the Olive Oil Pizza Dough (page 27); or 1 pound purchased fresh dough or frozen dough, thawed; or one 12- to 14-inch store-bought, prebaked plain pizza crust

2 tablespoons olive oil

1 medium shallot, minced

1 garlic clove, minced

1 cup peeled and chopped eggplant (about 1 small eggplant)

1 large globe or beefsteak tomato, chopped

1 small green bell pepper, cored, seeded, and chopped

1 tablespoon minced fresh rosemary or ½ tablespoon dried rosemary

1 tablespoon stemmed thyme leaves or 2 teaspoons dried thyme

½ teaspoon salt

½ teaspoon freshly ground black pepper

Up to ½ teaspoon red pepper flakes

6 ounces Gruyère, shredded

1½ ounces Parmigiano-Reggiano, finely grated

BAKING OPTIONS

With a pizza stone. Preheat the stone in the oven at 450°F for 30 to 45 minutes; or preheat the stone on a gas grill at medium, indirect heat (about 450°F) for 30

to 45 minutes; or build an indirect, medium-heat coal bed in a charcoal grill and preheat the stone for the same amount of time.

With a pizza tray or a large baking sheet. Preheat the oven to 450°F, a gas grill to indirect, medium heat (about 450°F), or build an indirect, medium-heat coal bed around the edge of a charcoal grill.

CRUST OPTIONS

Fresh dough on a pizza stone. Dust a pizza peel with flour, set the dough at its center, and dimple the dough with your fingertips until it's a flattened circle. Pick it up and shape it by holding its edge and rotating it slowly, stretching that edge all the while, until the circle is about 14 inches in diameter. Set the shaped dough floured side down on the peel.

Fresh dough on a pizza tray or a large baking sheet. Grease the tray or baking sheet with nonstick spray. Lay the dough at the center of either and dimple the dough with your fingertips—then pull and press it until it forms a 14-inch circle on the tray or an irregular rectangle, about 12×7 inches, on the baking sheet.

A prebaked crust. Place it on a floured pizza peel if using a pizza stone—or place the prebaked crust on a pizza tray or a large baking sheet.

1. Heat the olive oil in a large saucepan set over medium heat. Add the shallot and garlic; cook, stirring often, for 2 minutes.

2. Stir in the eggplant, tomato, bell pepper, rosemary, thyme, salt, pepper, and red pepper flakes (to taste); bring to a simmer, stirring often.

3. Cover, reduce the heat to low, and simmer until the vegetables are quite tender, about 30 minutes. Set aside to cool for 15 minutes.

4. Spread the shredded Gruyère evenly over the crust, leaving a ½-inch border at the edge. Spoon the eggplant mixture evenly over the cheese. Top with the grated Parmigiano-Reggiano.

5. Slide the crust from the peel onto the heated stone—or place the pie on its tray or baking sheet either in the oven or over the unheated portion of the grill. Bake or grill with the lid closed until the cheese is bubbling and the crust is somewhat firm to the touch, 18 to 20 minutes, checking on fresh dough occasionally so you can pop any air bubbles that may spring up across its surface. Slip the crust back onto the peel to remove it from the stone or transfer the hot pie on its tray or baking sheet to a wire cooling rack. In either case, cool for 5 minutes before slicing. If you like, slide the pie from the peel, tray, or baking sheet right onto the wire rack after a minute or so to ensure that the crust doesn't steam against a solid surface.

Lorraine Pizza

Modeled on the quiche of the same name, this pizza topping is a thick, luscious mixture of bacon, cheese, and red onion, set over a rich, cream-laced sauce. Use only slab bacon, sometimes sold with the thick rind, which must first be removed.

MAKES 1 PIZZA

Either all-purpose flour for the pizza peel or nonstick spray for the baking sheet

One recipe homemade dough, preferably the Semolina Pizza Dough (page 29); or 1 pound purchased fresh dough or frozen dough, thawed; or one 12- to 14-inch store-bought, prebaked plain pizza crust

5 ounces slab bacon, diced

1 large egg, at room temperature

1 tablespoon heavy or whipping cream

8 ounces (½ pound) Swiss, Emmental, Gruyère, or Muenster, shredded

¼ cup diced red onion

2 teaspoons stemmed thyme leaves

BAKING OPTIONS

With a pizza stone. Preheat the stone in the oven at 450°F for 30 to 45 minutes; or preheat the stone on a gas grill at medium, indirect heat (about 450°F) for 30 to 45 minutes; or build an indirect, medium-heat coal bed in a charcoal grill and preheat the stone for the same amount of time.

With a pizza tray or a large baking sheet. Preheat the oven to 450°F, a gas grill to indirect, medium heat (about 450°F), or build an indirect, medium-heat coal bed around the edge of a charcoal grill.

CRUST OPTIONS

Fresh dough on a pizza stone. As always, dust a pizza peel with flour, then set the dough at its center. Dimple the dough with your fingertips into a thick, flattened circle; pick it up and shape it with your hands, holding its edge, slowly turning the dough until it's about 14 inches in diameter. Set it floured side down on the peel.

Fresh dough on a pizza tray or a large baking sheet. Grease either with nonstick spray. Lay the dough on the tray or baking sheet and dimple the dough with your fingertips—then pull and press the dough until it forms a 14-inch circle on the tray or a 12 × 7-inch irregular rectangle on the baking sheet.

A prebaked crust. Place it on a floured pizza peel if using a pizza stone—or place the prebaked crust on a pizza tray or a large baking sheet.

1. Place the diced bacon in a large skillet set over medium heat and cook until soft and just beginning to brown.

2. Beat the egg and cream in a small bowl with an electric mixer at medium speed until thick and fairly creamy, then spread this mixture evenly on the crust, keeping it back ½ inch from the edge.

3. Top the pie with the shredded cheese, then dot with the partially fried bacon bits. Sprinkle the diced onion and thyme evenly over the top.

4. Slip the crust from the peel to the heated stone or place the pie on its tray or baking sheet either in the oven or over the unheated portion of the grill. Bake or grill with the lid closed until the cheese is bubbling and the crust has turned golden brown, 16 to 18 minutes. Slide the peel back under the pizza to remove it from the very hot stone—or transfer the pie on its tray or baking sheet to a wire rack. Cool for 5 minutes before slicing. To ensure a crisp crust, transfer the pie from the peel, tray, or baking sheet directly to the wire rack after a minute or two.

Clams, Sausage, and Hazelnuts Pizza

There are several ways to get the clams for this Spanish-inspired pie: (1) buy canned clams; (2) buy 10 ounces of fresh, shucked clams at the seafood counter and sauté them in a little olive oil over medium heat until tender before chopping into small pieces; or (3) steam whole fresh clams and shuck them once they've opened. To do the latter, place 16 to 20 medium clams in 1 inch of simmering water in a large, covered saucepan set over medium heat; cover and cook just until they open, about 7 minutes. Cool slightly, then remove the meat from the shells and chop it into bite-sized pieces.

MAKES 1 PIZZA

All-purpose flour to dust the pizza peel or olive oil to grease the pizza tray or a large baking sheet

One recipe homemade dough, preferably the Olive Oil Pizza Dough (page 27); or 1 pound purchased fresh dough or frozen dough, thawed; or one 12- to 14-inch store-bought, prebaked plain pizza crust

6 ounces Manchego or other dry, hard cheese, preferably a Spanish sheep's milk cheese, shredded

1 small red onion, diced (about ¾ cup)

½ teaspoon smoked sweet paprika

4 ounces (¼ pound) dried Spanish chorizo (see page 209), diced

One 10-ounce can chopped baby clams, drained and rinsed

6 tablespoons chopped, toasted, skinned hazelnuts

BAKING OPTIONS

With a pizza stone. Preheat the stone in the oven at 450°F for 30 to 45 minutes; or preheat the stone on a gas grill at medium, indirect heat (about 450°F) for 30 to 45 minutes; or build an indirect, medium-heat coal bed in a charcoal grill and preheat the stone for the same amount of time.

With a pizza tray or a baking sheet. Preheat the oven to 450°F, a gas grill to indirect, medium heat (about 450°F), or build an indirect, medium-heat coal bed around the edge of a charcoal grill.

CRUST OPTIONS

Fresh dough on a pizza stone. Dust the pizza peel with flour, then set the dough at its center. Dimple the dough with your fingertips, then pick it up by its edge and shape it into a circle about 14 inches in diameter. Set it floured side down on the peel.

Fresh dough on a pizza tray or a large baking sheet. Use a little olive oil on a piece of paper towel to grease a pizza tray or a large baking sheet. Lay the dough on the tray or baking sheet; dimple it into a flattened round with your fingertips. Then pull and press it until it forms a 14-inch circle or a 12 × 7-inch somewhat irregular rectangle on the baking sheet.

A prebaked crust. Place it on a floured pizza peel if using a pizza stone—or place the prebaked crust right on a pizza tray or a large baking sheet.

1. Spread the crust with the shredded cheese, taking care to leave a ½-inch border at the crust's edge.

2. Mix the onion with the smoked paprika in a small bowl, then sprinkle over the cheese along with the diced sausage. Sprinkle the clams evenly over the pizza, followed by the hazelnuts.

3. Slide the crust from the peel to the heated stone—or place the pie on the pizza tray or the baking sheet in the oven or over the unheated portion of the grill grate. Bake or grill with the lid closed until the cheese has melted and the crust is golden brown but also a little firm to the touch, 16 to 18 minutes. Slide the peel back under the pizza to take it off the very hot stone—or transfer the pie on the pizza tray or the baking sheet to a wire rack. Cool for 5 minutes before slicing.

Picadillo Pizza

Picadillo is a spicy ground-beef mixture, served in lettuce wraps or on top of rice and beans. This aromatic mixture has flashed across the world; there are now Vietnamese and Indonesian versions, but this pizza topping adheres closely to its Latin American origins. Spice it up with more jalapeños, if you like.

MAKES 1 PIZZA

Yellow cornmeal for the pizza peel or olive oil for the pizza tray or the baking sheet

One recipe homemade dough, preferably the Classic Pizza Dough (page 23) or the Cracker Pizza Dough (page 35); or 1 pound purchased fresh dough or frozen dough, thawed; or one 12- to 14-inch store-bought, prebaked plain pizza crust

1 tablespoon olive oil

4 garlic cloves, minced

½ pound lean ground beef, veal, or turkey

1 large plum tomato, chopped

1 hard-cooked egg, peeled and chopped (see Note)

1 medium scallion, minced

5 tablespoons minced parsley leaves or cilantro leaves

¼ cup chopped pitted green olives

2 tablespoons chopped golden raisins, dried pineapple, or dried apple

2 teaspoons minced oregano leaves or 1 teaspoon dried oregano

2 teaspoons Worcestershire sauce

½ teaspoon salt

½ teaspoon freshly ground black pepper

Several minced jarred pickled jalapeño slices

6 ounces manchego, shredded

BAKING OPTIONS

With a pizza stone. Preheat the stone in the oven at 450°F for 30 to 45 minutes; or preheat the stone on a gas grill at medium, indirect heat (about 450°F) for 30 to 45 minutes; or build an indirect, medium-heat coal bed in a charcoal grill and preheat the stone for the same amount of time.

With a pizza tray or a large baking sheet. Preheat the oven to 450°F, a gas grill to indirect, medium heat (about 450°F), or build an indirect, medium-heat coal bed around the edge of a charcoal grill.

CRUST OPTIONS

Fresh dough on a pizza stone. Dust a pizza peel with cornmeal, set the dough at its center, and form the dough into a large circle by dimpling it with your fingertips. Pick up the dough by its edge and shape it by rotating it and gently stretching it until it's about 14 inches in diameter. If using the Cracker Pizza Dough, it's too fragile to be picked up and shaped; see the special instructions on page 35. In any event, return the shaped dough cornmeal side down to the peel.

Fresh dough on a pizza tray or a large baking sheet. Grease the tray or baking sheet with some olive oil on a paper towel. Lay the dough at the center of the tray or baking sheet; dimple the dough with your fingertips until it's a flattened circle—then pull and press it until it forms a 14-inch circle on the pizza tray or an irregular 12 × 7-inch rectangle on the baking sheet.

A prebaked crust. Place it on a pizza peel if using a pizza stone—or place the prebaked crust on a pizza tray or a large baking sheet.

1. Heat a large skillet over medium heat, then swirl in the olive oil. Add the garlic and cook for 30 seconds, stirring constantly.

2. Add the ground meat; cook, stirring often, until well browned and cooked through, 4 to 5 minutes. Remove the skillet from the heat. Hold the ground beef and garlic to one side of the skillet with a wooden spoon and drain off any fat.

3. Stir in the tomato, egg, and scallion. Gently stir in 3 tablespoons of the chopped parsley or cilantro, the olives, dried fruit, oregano, Worcestershire sauce, salt, pepper, and minced jalapeños (to taste).

4. Top the prepared crust with the shredded manchego, taking care to leave a ½-inch border at the crust's edge. Spoon and spread the ground-beef mixture over the pizza.

5. Slide the pizza from the peel to the hot stone or place the pizza tray or the baking sheet either in the oven or over the unheated portion of the grill grate. Bake or grill with the lid closed until the crust has turned golden brown at its edge and has begun to firm up all around, 16 to 18 minutes, popping any air bubbles that may appear on fresh dough during the first 10 minutes in the oven or on the grill.

6. Slip the peel back under the pie, taking care not to jostle the topping, so you can take the pizza off the stone to cool for 5 minutes—or transfer the pie on its tray or the baking sheet to a wire rack to cool for the same amount of time. Top the pizza with the remaining 2 tablespoons chopped parsley or cilantro. You can use one herb in the cooked filling and the other as the fresh topping—or the same in both. Slice into wedges to serve.

NOTE: To hard-cook an egg, place it in a small saucepan and cover with water to a depth of 1 inch. Cover and bring to a full boil over medium-high heat. Remove from the heat and set aside, covered, for 16 minutes. Drain and rinse with cool water until room temperature, even a little chilled. Roll the egg along your work surface to fracture the shell before peeling and chopping. Or go the easy route: look for chopped hard-cooked egg at the salad bar of your supermarket. You'll need about ¼ cup.

Stir-Fry Pizza

Soy cheese has the right mild taste to complement this pizza-style version of an Asian stir-fry. The pizza is baked at a slightly lower temperature so the pork doesn't turn rubbery.

MAKES 1 PIZZA

All-purpose flour for the pizza peel or peanut oil for the pizza tray or the
   baking sheet
One recipe homemade dough, preferably the Classic Pizza Dough (page 23);
   or 1 pound purchased fresh dough or frozen dough, thawed; or one 12- to
   14-inch store-bought, prebaked plain pizza crust
8 ounces (½ pound) trimmed pork loin, cut into thin rounds and then into
   matchsticks
1½ tablespoons soy sauce
1 tablespoon rice vinegar
2 tablespoons toasted sesame oil
6 tablespoons dark Chinese condiment sauce, preferably bean sauce, hoisin
   sauce, chou hee sauce, or Chinese barbecue sauce
4 ounces (¼ pound) soy mozzarella, shredded
2 cups chopped mixed quick-cooking vegetables, such as onions, scallions,
   zucchini, canned baby corn, canned sliced water chestnuts, seeded bell
   peppers, or peeled eggplant
1 tablespoon sesame seeds

BAKING OPTIONS

With a pizza stone. Position the rack in the middle of the oven and preheat the stone in the oven at 450°F for 30 to 45 minutes; or preheat the stone on a gas grill at medium, indirect heat (about 450°F) for 30 to 45 minutes; or build an

indirect, medium-heat coal bed in a charcoal grill and then preheat the stone for the same amount of time.

With a pizza tray or a large baking sheet. Preheat the oven to 450°F, a gas grill to indirect, medium heat (about 450°F), or build an indirect, medium-heat fire around the edge of a charcoal grill.

CRUST OPTIONS

Fresh dough on a pizza stone. Dust a pizza peel with flour, set the dough at its center, and dimple the dough into a flat, thick circle with your fingertips. Pick it up, hold its edge with both hands, and slowly rotate the dough, stretching it gently at the edge all the while, until the circle is about 14 inches in diameter. Set it floured side down on the peel.

Fresh dough on a pizza tray or a large baking sheet. Grease the tray or baking sheet with a little peanut oil on a piece of paper towel. Lay the dough at the center of either and dimple the dough into a flat, thick circle with your fingertips—then pull and press it until it forms a 14-inch circle on the tray or an irregular rectangle, about 12 × 7 inches, on the baking sheet.

A prebaked crust. Place it on a floured pizza peel if using a pizza stone—or place the prebaked crust on a pizza tray or a large baking sheet.

1. Toss the pork with 1 tablespoon of the soy sauce and the rice vinegar in a large bowl; set aside for 10 minutes.

2. Heat 1 tablespoon sesame oil in a large skillet over medium heat. Add the pork and cook, stirring often, until cooked through and well browned, 2 to 3 minutes. Set aside.

3. Spread the dark Chinese condiment sauce over the crust, keeping it back about ½ inch from the crust's edge. Sprinkle the shredded soy cheese evenly over the sauce.

4. Top with the chopped vegetables, spreading them evenly over the crust; then arrange the cooked pork over the pie. Sprinkle the crust with the remaining 1 tablespoon sesame oil and the sesame seeds.

5. Slip the crust from the peel onto the heated stone or place the pizza tray or the baking sheet with the pie in the oven or over the unheated section of the grill grate. Bake or grill with the lid closed until the cheese has melted and the crust is golden brown, popping any air bubbles that may come up on fresh dough, about 18 minutes.

6. Slip the peel back under the crust to take it off the stone or transfer the pizza on its tray or baking sheet to a wire rack. Set aside to cool for 5 minutes. Drizzle with the remaining ½ tablespoon soy sauce before slicing and serving.

Peking Duck Pizza

Peking duck, a Chinese restaurant favorite, has been a Beijing specialty since the early 1300s—so much of a specialty that there were once imperial strictures as to the life span of the duck and the exactitudes of the preparation. Truth be told, they matter little to a quick pizza that's a nice go-along with cocktails or a summery dinner on its own. Get a precooked duck from a Chinese restaurant or market.

MAKES 1 PIZZA

All-purpose flour to dust the pizza peel or nonstick spray to grease the pizza
   tray or a large baking sheet
One recipe homemade dough, preferably the Classic Pizza Dough (page 23);
   or 1 pound purchased fresh dough or frozen dough, thawed; or one 12- to
   14-inch store-bought, prebaked plain pizza crust
1 tablespoon toasted sesame oil
3 tablespoons hoisin sauce (see Note)
2 cups skinned, defatted Chinese roast duck meat, chopped (about 8 ounces),
   plus ½ cup skin shredded and reserved
1 cup thinly sliced scallions

BAKING OPTIONS

With a pizza stone. Preheat the stone in the oven at 450°F for 30 to 45 minutes; or preheat the stone on a gas grill at medium, indirect heat (about 450°F) for 30 to 45 minutes; or build an indirect, medium-heat coal bed in a charcoal grill and preheat the stone for the same amount of time.

With a pizza tray or a large baking sheet. Preheat the oven to 450°F, a gas grill to indirect, medium heat (about 450°F), or build an indirect, medium-heat coal bed around the edge of a charcoal grill.

CRUST OPTIONS

Fresh dough on a pizza stone. Dust a pizza peel with flour. Then add the dough and form it into a large circle by dimpling it with your fingertips. Pick it up, hold it by its edge, and shape it by rotating it slowly and stretching it gently until it's a circle about 14 inches in diameter. Set it floured side down on the peel.

Fresh dough baked on a pizza tray or a large baking sheet. Grease the tray or baking sheet lightly with nonstick spray. Lay the dough at its center and dimple the dough with your fingertips—then pull and press it until it forms a 14-inch circle on the tray or a 12 × 7-inch irregular rectangle on the baking sheet.

A prebaked crust. Place it on a pizza peel if using a pizza stone—or place the prebaked crust on a pizza tray or a large baking sheet.

1. Spread the sesame oil evenly over the crust.

2. Slip the crust from the peel onto the stone or place it on the tray or the baking sheet in the oven or on the grill over indirect heat. Bake or grill for 7 minutes. Slip the peel back under the crust and remove it from the stone—or transfer the pie on its tray or baking sheet to a wire rack.

3. Spread the hoisin sauce over the crust, leaving a ½-inch border at the edge. Lay the pieces of duck meat evenly over the sauce, then sprinkle the scallions on top. Finally, lay the shreds of duck skin evenly over the pie.

4. Use the peel to return the pizza to the stone or use a mitt to put the still-hot tray or the baking sheet back in the oven or on the grill over indirect heat. Continue to bake or grill over indirect heat until the crust is golden brown and the duck skin is sizzling and crisp, about 8 minutes. Again, use the peel to remove the pizza from the stone and set aside, or once again transfer the pie on the tray or the baking sheet to a wire rack. Cool for 5 minutes before slicing and serving.

To ensure a crisp crust, transfer the pie from the peel, tray, or baking sheet right onto the wire rack after a minute or two.

NOTE: For a more pungent taste, try hoisin's stronger-tasting kin, chou hee sauce, available at most specialty Chinese or Southeast Asian markets.

TWENTY-THREE MODERN PIES

Pizza has moved well beyond a narrow range of flavors. Today, there are all sorts of pies—and we're not above jumping into the fray with tweaked versions of classics (the Polynesian Pizza, page 233), with pies that are unique if whimsical (the Duck Confit Pizza, page 215), and with pies that are comfort food of a decidedly homey stripe (the Pot Pie Pizza, page 236, or the Peas and Carrots Pizza, page 227).

The sky's the limit. Here, in alphabetical order, are newfangled favorites, a gamut of flavors in a set of main-course pies.

Barbecue Chicken Pizza

Bottled barbecue sauce makes an excellent pizza sauce—and one that's endlessly variable, too, whether tangy or savory, sweet or spicy hot, depending on the kind you buy. That said, there's no reason to buy an excessively smoky sauce because this recipe also calls for smoked provolone or Swiss.

MAKES 1 PIZZA

Either all-purpose flour for the pizza peel or nonstick spray for the baking sheet

One recipe homemade dough, preferably the Classic Pizza Dough (page 23); or 1 pound purchased fresh dough or frozen dough, thawed; or one 12- to 14-inch store-bought, prebaked plain pizza crust

6 tablespoons barbecue sauce (use any variety you prefer, hot to mild)

4 ounces (¼ pound) smoked provolone or smoked Swiss, shredded

1 cup chopped, cooked chicken meat (see page 147)

½ small red onion, diced (about ½ cup)

1 teaspoon minced oregano leaves or ½ teaspoon dried oregano

1 ounce Parmigiano-Reggiano, finely grated

½ teaspoon red pepper flakes, optional

BAKING OPTIONS

With a pizza stone. Preheat the stone in the oven at 450°F for 30 to 45 minutes; or preheat the stone on a gas grill at medium, indirect heat (about 450°F) for 30 to 45 minutes; or build an indirect, medium-heat coal bed in a charcoal grill and preheat the stone for the same amount of time.

With a baking sheet. Preheat the oven to 450°F, a gas grill to indirect, medium heat (about 450°F), or build an indirect, medium-heat coal bed around the edge of a charcoal grill.

CRUST OPTIONS

Fresh dough on a pizza stone. First, lightly dust a pizza peel with flour. Add the dough and form it into a large circle by first dimpling it with your fingertips, then picking it up by its edge and shaping it with your hands into a circle about 14 inches in diameter. Set the dough floured side down onto the peel.

Fresh dough on a pizza tray or a large baking sheet. Grease either with nonstick spray and lay the dough in a mound at the center of the tray or baking sheet. Dimple the dough with your fingertips, then pull and press the dough until it forms a circle about 14 inches in diameter on the tray or an irregular rectangle, about 13 × 7 inches, on the baking sheet.

A prebaked crust. Place it on a pizza peel if using a pizza stone—or place the prebaked crust right on a pizza tray or a large baking sheet.

1. Use a rubber spatula to spread the barbecue sauce evenly over the prepared dough, leaving a ¹⁄₂-inch border at the edge. Top with the shredded, smoked cheese.

2. Arrange the chicken pieces over the cheese, then sprinkle with the diced onion and oregano.

3. Top with the grated Parmigiano-Reggiano and the red pepper flakes, if using. Slide the pie from the peel to the very hot stone—or place the pizza tray or the baking sheet with its pie either right in the oven or on the portion of the grill's grate that is not directly over the heat source.

4. Bake or grill with the lid closed until the crust is golden and the cheese has melted and even begun to brown lightly, 16 to 18 minutes. Slip the peel back under the crust to remove it from the stone or transfer the pizza tray or the baking sheet with the pie to a wire rack. Set the pie aside to cool for 5 minutes before slicing and serving.

Beef and Mushroom Pizza

Break out the beer or iced tea. Like the all-American casserole favorite, this pizza combines ground beef, sautéed mushrooms, and softened onions. And the sauce underneath it all? Bottled steak sauce, of course.

MAKES 1 PIZZA

All-purpose flour for dusting the pizza peel or nonstick spray for greasing the pizza tray or a large baking sheet

One recipe homemade dough, preferably the Classic Pizza Dough (page 23); or 1 pound purchased fresh dough or frozen dough, thawed; or one 12- to 14-inch store-bought, prebaked plain pizza crust

1 tablespoon unsalted butter

1 small yellow onion, chopped (about ½ cup)

5 ounces cremini or white button mushrooms, thinly sliced (about 1½ cups)

8 ounces (½ pound) lean ground beef

2 tablespoons dry sherry, dry vermouth, or dry white wine

1 tablespoon minced parsley leaves

2 teaspoons Worcestershire sauce

1 teaspoon stemmed thyme leaves or ½ teaspoon dried thyme

1 teaspoon minced sage leaves or ½ teaspoon dried sage

½ teaspoon salt

½ teaspoon freshly ground black pepper

2 tablespoons bottled steak sauce

6 ounces Cheddar, shredded

BAKING OPTIONS

With a pizza stone. Preheat the stone in the oven at 450°F for 30 to 45 minutes; or preheat the stone on a gas grill at medium, indirect heat (about 450°F) for 30 to 45 minutes; or build an indirect, medium-heat coal bed in a charcoal grill and preheat the stone for the same amount of time.

With a pizza tray or a large baking sheet. Preheat the oven to 450°F, a gas grill to indirect, medium heat (about 450°F), or build an indirect, medium-heat coal bed around the edge of a charcoal grill.

CRUST OPTIONS

Fresh dough on a pizza stone. Dust a pizza peel with flour. Set the dough on it and use your fingertips to dimple the dough into a large circle. Pick up the dough by its edge and turn it in your hands until it's a circle about 14 inches in diameter. Set the shaped dough floured side down on the peel.

Fresh dough on a pizza tray or a large baking sheet. Grease either with nonstick spray. Lay the dough on the tray or baking sheet; dimple it with your fingertips—then pull and press it until it forms a 14-inch circle on the tray or an irregular 12 × 7-inch rectangle on the baking sheet.

A prebaked crust. Place it on a pizza peel if using a pizza stone—or place the prebaked crust right on a pizza tray or a large baking sheet.

1. Melt the butter in a large skillet set over medium heat. Add the onion; cook, stirring often, until softened, about 2 minutes.

2. Add the mushrooms; continue cooking, stirring occasionally, until they soften, give off their liquid, and it evaporates to a glaze, about 5 minutes.

3. Crumble in the ground beef; cook, stirring occasionally, until well browned and cooked through, about 4 minutes.

4. Stir in the sherry, or its substitute, the parsley, Worcestershire sauce, thyme, sage, salt, and pepper. Continue cooking, stirring constantly, until the skillet is again dry. Set aside off the heat.

5. Spread the steak sauce evenly over the crust, leaving a ½-inch border at the edge. Top with the shredded Cheddar, keeping that border clean.

6. Spoon and spread the ground beef mixture evenly over the cheese. Then slip the pizza from the peel to the hot stone—or place the pie on its pizza tray or baking sheet either in the oven or over the unheated portion of the grill grate.

7. Bake or grill with the lid closed until the cheese has begun to bubble and the crust is brown at its edge and somewhat firm to the touch, 16 to 18 minutes. Make sure you pop any air bubbles that arise on fresh dough, particularly at the edge and particularly during the first 10 minutes of baking. Slide the peel back under the crust, taking care not to dislodge the topping, and then set aside for 5 minutes—or place the pizza on the pizza tray or the baking sheet on a wire rack for the same amount of time before slicing and serving. Because the toppings are especially heavy, it may not be possible to remove the pizza easily from the peel, tray, or baking sheet before slicing. If using a nonstick tray or baking sheet, carefully transfer the whole pie to a cutting board to avoid nicking the nonstick surface.

Broccoli and Cheese Sauce Pizza

Here's a pizza that replicates a casserole favorite. The dough must be completely baked before it is topped because the cheese sauce is so thick, it will keep the crust from getting crispy.

MAKES 1 PIZZA

All-purpose flour for dusting a pizza peel or nonstick spray for greasing a pizza tray or a large baking sheet

One recipe homemade dough, preferably the Classic Pizza Dough (page 23) or the Parmesan Pizza Dough (page 31); or 1 pound purchased fresh dough or frozen dough, thawed; or one 12- to 14-inch store-bought, prebaked plain pizza crust

2 tablespoons unsalted butter

2 tablespoons all-purpose flour

1¼ cups regular, low-fat, or fat-free milk

6 ounces Cheddar, shredded

1 teaspoon Dijon mustard

1 teaspoon stemmed thyme leaves or ½ teaspoon dried thyme

½ teaspoon salt

Several dashes hot red pepper sauce

3 cups fresh broccoli florets, steamed; or frozen broccoli florets, thawed (see Note)

2 ounces Parmigiano-Reggiano or Grana Padano, finely grated

BAKING OPTIONS

With a pizza stone. Preheat the stone in the oven at 450°F for 30 to 45 minutes; or preheat the stone on a gas grill at medium, indirect heat (about 450°F) for 30 to 45 minutes; or build an indirect, medium-heat coal bed in a charcoal grill and preheat the stone for the same amount of time.

With a pizza tray or a baking sheet. Preheat the oven to 450°F, a gas grill to indirect, medium heat (about 450°F), or build an indirect, medium-heat coal bed around the edge of a charcoal grill.

CRUST OPTIONS

Fresh dough on a pizza stone. Dust a pizza peel with flour. Place the dough in the peel's center and form the dough into a large circle by dimpling it with your fingertips. Pick up the dough and rotate it by holding its edge, pulling it slightly as you do so, until the crust is a circle about 14 inches in diameter. Set it floured side down on the peel.

Fresh dough on a pizza tray or a large baking sheet. Grease one or the other with nonstick spray. Lay the dough on the tray or baking sheet; dimple the dough with your fingertips until it's a flattened circle. Pull and press the dough until it forms a 14-inch circle on the tray or an irregular rectangle, about 12 × 7 inches, on the baking sheet.

A prebaked crust. Place it on a floured pizza peel if using a pizza stone—or place the prebaked crust right on a pizza tray or large baking sheet.

1. Melt the butter in a large saucepan set over medium heat. Whisk in the flour until smooth and the resulting mixture becomes very light blond, about 1 minute.

2. Reduce the heat to medium-low and whisk in the milk, pouring it in a slow, steady stream into the butter and flour mixture. Continue whisking over the heat until thickened, like melted ice cream, perhaps a little thinner, about 3 minutes or at the first sign of a simmer.

3. Remove the pan from the heat and whisk in the shredded Cheddar, mustard, thyme, salt, and hot red pepper sauce (to taste). Cool for 10 to 15 minutes, whisking occasionally.

4. If you're working with a prebaked crust, skip this step. If you're using fresh dough, slide the shaped but not yet topped crust from the peel to the hot stone or place the crust on its tray or baking sheet either in the oven or over the un-heated portion of the grill grate. Bake or grill with the lid closed until the crust is light brown, taking care to pop any air bubbles that arise across its surface or at its edge, about 12 minutes. Slide the peel back under the crust to remove it from the stone—or transfer the pizza tray or the baking sheet with the crust to a wire rack.

5. Spread the thick cheese sauce over the crust, leaving a ½-inch border at the edge. Top with the broccoli florets, arranging them evenly over the sauce. Sprinkle with the grated Parmigiano-Reggiano.

6. Place the topped pizza on the stone or set the pie on its tray or baking sheet in the oven or the unheated section of the grill. Bake or grill until the cheese sauce is bubbling, about 12 minutes. Again slide the peel under the pie or transfer the pizza tray or baking sheet with the pie to the wire rack. Cool for 5 minutes before slicing.

NOTE: If using fresh broccoli florets, steam them over 1 inch of simmering water until crisp-tender. Set a vegetable steamer in a large pot with the right amount of water, bring to a simmer over high heat, add the broccoli, cover, reduce the heat to low, and steam 2 minutes. Immediately transfer the florets to a colander set in the sink and refresh under cool water until room temperature.

Broccoli and Tomato Sauce Pizza

While we suggest a healthy dose of red pepper flakes for this hearty pie, you can up the amount to even 2 teaspoons, depending on your taste. More is definitely better—if you like the heat. (See the Note on page 200 for directions on how to steam the broccoli florets.)

MAKES 1 PIZZA

Either yellow cornmeal for dusting a pizza peel or olive oil for greasing a pizza tray or a large baking sheet

One recipe homemade dough, preferably the Classic Pizza Dough (page 23) or the Spelt Pizza Dough (page 33); or 1 pound purchased fresh dough or frozen dough, thawed; or one 12- to 14-inch store-bought, prebaked plain pizza crust

1 large jarred pimiento or roasted red pepper (see Note)

½ teaspoon red pepper flakes

½ cup Classic Pizza Sauce (page 38), No-Cook Pizza Sauce (page 39), or jarred plain pizza sauce

3 ounces mozzarella, shredded

3 ounces provolone, Muenster, or Havarti, shredded

2 cups frozen broccoli florets or fresh florets, steamed

1 ounce Parmigiano-Reggiano or Grana Padano, finely grated

BAKING OPTIONS

With a pizza stone. Preheat the stone in the oven at 450°F for 30 to 45 minutes; or preheat the stone on a gas grill at medium, indirect heat (about 450°F) for 30 to 45 minutes; or build an indirect, medium-heat coal bed in a charcoal grill and preheat the stone for the same amount of time.

With a pizza tray or a baking sheet. Preheat the oven to 450°F, a gas grill to indirect, medium heat (about 450°F), or build an indirect, medium-heat fire around the edge of a charcoal grill.

CRUST OPTIONS

Fresh dough on a pizza stone. Dust a pizza peel with cornmeal. Place the dough as a lump on the peel and then dimple it with your fingertips until it's a large circle. Pick up the dough, hold it by its edge in both hands, and rotate it, stretching slightly, until it's a circle about 14 inches in diameter. Set it cornmeal side down on the peel. If you've used the Spelt Pizza Dough, it may be too fragile to shape with this technique; see page 34 for specific instructions related to its shaping.

Fresh dough on a pizza tray or a large baking sheet. Grease the tray or baking sheet with olive oil. Lay the dough on either and dimple it with your fingertips—then pull and press the dough until it forms a 14-inch circle on the tray or an irregular rectangle, 13 inches long by 7 inches wide, on the baking sheet.

A prebaked crust. Place it on a floured pizza peel if using a pizza stone—or place the prebaked crust right on a pizza tray or a large baking sheet.

1. Puree the pimiento with the red pepper flakes in a mini food processor until smooth. Alternatively, grind them in a mortar with a pestle until a smooth paste. Set aside.

2. Spread the pizza sauce evenly over the prepared crust, leaving a ½-inch border at the edge. Top with both shredded cheeses, keeping that border intact.

3. Sprinkle the broccoli florets around the pie, again leaving that border intact. Dot the pimiento puree over the top, using about 1 teaspoon for each dollop. Top with the finely grated Parmigiano-Reggiano. Carefully slide the pizza from the peel onto the hot stone—or if you've used a pizza tray or baking sheet, place either with its pie in the oven or over the unheated portion of the grill grate.

4. Bake or grill with the lid closed until the cheese has melted, the red sauce is thick, and the crust is golden brown and firm to the touch, 16 to 18 minutes.

Either slip the peel back under the pizza to take it off the very hot stone or transfer the pizza on its tray or baking sheet to a wire rack. If you want to ensure the crust stays crisp, remove the pie from the peel, tray, or baking sheet after it's cooled for about 1 minute; place the pizza directly on the wire rack. In any case, cool for a total of 5 minutes before slicing.

NOTE: Don't blot the pimiento or roasted red pepper dry; wet, it will puree into a smooth paste.

Buffalo Chicken Pizza

No, there are no wings here; but the chicken is cooked in butter, the whole pie is topped with a chile-laced sauce, and blue cheese rounds out the whole shebang. Did someone mention a bottle of dark beer?

MAKES 1 PIZZA

Either yellow cornmeal to dust a pizza peel or unsalted butter to grease a
   pizza tray or a large baking sheet
One recipe homemade dough, preferably the Classic Pizza Dough (page 23);
   or 1 pound purchased fresh dough or frozen dough, thawed; or one 12- to
   14-inch store-bought, prebaked plain pizza crust
1 tablespoon unsalted butter
10 ounces boneless skinless chicken breasts, thinly sliced
1 tablespoon hot red pepper sauce, preferably Tabasco
1 tablespoon Worcestershire sauce
6 tablespoons bottled chile sauce, such as Heinz
3 ounces mozzarella, shredded
3 ounces Monterey Jack, shredded
3 medium celery ribs, thinly sliced
2 ounces blue cheese, such as Gorgonzola, Danish blue, or Roquefort

BAKING OPTIONS

With a pizza stone. Preheat the stone in the oven at 450°F for 30 to 45 minutes; or preheat the stone on a gas grill at medium, indirect heat (about 450°F) for 30 to 45 minutes; or build an indirect, medium-heat coal bed in a charcoal grill and preheat the stone for the same amount of time.

With a pizza tray or a large baking sheet. Preheat the oven to 450°F, a gas grill to indirect, medium heat (about 450°F), or build an indirect, medium-heat coal bed around the edge of a charcoal grill.

CRUST OPTIONS

Fresh dough on a pizza stone. Dust a pizza peel with cornmeal. Place the dough in the peel's center and form the dough into a large circle by dimpling it with your fingertips. Pick up the dough and shape it with your hands, holding its edge, slowly turning the dough until it's a circle about 14 inches in diameter. Set it cornmeal side down on the peel.

Fresh dough on a baking sheet. Smear a little unsalted butter on a paper towel, then rub this around a pizza tray or a large baking sheet to grease it thoroughly. Lay the dough on the tray or baking sheet; dimple the dough with your fingertips until it's a flattened circle. Then pull and press it until it forms a 14-inch circle on the tray or an irregular 12 × 7-inch rectangle on the baking sheet.

A prebaked crust. Place it on a cornmeal-dusted pizza peel if using a pizza stone—or place the prebaked crust on a buttered pizza tray or large baking sheet.

1. Melt the butter in a large skillet or wok set over medium heat. Add the sliced chicken; cook, stirring often, until cooked through, about 5 minutes. Remove the skillet or wok from the heat and stir in the hot red pepper sauce and the Worcestershire sauce.

2. Spread the chile sauce over the crust, taking care to leave a ½-inch border at the edge. Lay the coated sliced chicken over the sauce.

3. Top with the shredded mozzarella and Monterey Jack, preserving the edge of the crust. Sprinkle the sliced celery evenly over the pie. Finally, crumble the blue cheese evenly in little dribs and drabs all over the other toppings.

4. Slip the pie from the peel to the hot stone—or place the pie on its pizza tray or baking sheet either in the oven or over the unheated section of the grill grate. Bake or grill with the lid closed until the cheese has melted and is starting to brown across the pie, 16 to 18 minutes. The crust should be somewhat firm to the touch—and any air bubbles that arise on fresh dough while baking should be immediately popped. Slide the peel back under the pie—watch out: the stone is hot—and then set aside to cool for 5 minutes, or remove the tray or baking sheet from the oven and let the pizza cool on a wire rack for 5 minutes before slicing and serving. For a crisp crust, transfer the pie after a minute or so from the peel, tray, or baking sheet directly onto the wire rack to cool a bit before slicing.

Chard and Blue Cheese Pizza

Chard is a leafy green, a power pack of nutrition. Cut out and discard the thick, tough, fibrous stems before shredding the leaves.

MAKES 1 PIZZA

Yellow cornmeal for the peel or nonstick spray for the pizza tray or baking sheet

One recipe homemade dough, preferably the Classic Pizza Dough (page 23); or 1 pound purchased fresh dough or frozen dough, thawed; or one 12- to 14-inch store-bought, prebaked plain pizza crust

2 tablespoons unsalted butter

3 garlic cloves, minced

4 cups tightly packed, shredded, stemmed Swiss chard leaves

6 ounces mozzarella, shredded

⅓ cup crumbled Gorgonzola, Danish blue, or Roquefort

½ teaspoon grated nutmeg

Up to ½ teaspoon red pepper flakes, optional

BAKING OPTIONS

With a pizza stone. Preheat the stone in the oven at 450°F for 30 to 45 minutes; or preheat the stone on a gas grill at medium, indirect heat (about 450°F) for 30 to 45 minutes; or build an indirect, medium-heat coal bed in a charcoal grill and preheat the stone for the same amount of time.

With a pizza tray or a large baking sheet. Preheat the oven to 450°F, a gas grill to indirect, medium heat (about 450°F), or build an indirect, medium-heat coal bed around the edge of a charcoal grill.

CRUST OPTIONS

Fresh pizza dough on a pizza stone. Dust a pizza peel with cornmeal, then set the dough at its center. Form it into a large circle by dimpling it with your fingertips. Pick it up and shape it with your hands, holding its edge, slowly turning the dough until it's about 14 inches in diameter. Set it floured side down on the peel.

Fresh dough on a pizza tray or a large baking sheet. Grease either one with non-stick spray. Lay the dough on the tray or baking sheet and dimple the dough with your fingertips—then pull and press it until it forms a 14-inch circle on the tray or a 12 × 7-inch irregular rectangle on the baking sheet.

A prebaked crust. Place it on a pizza peel if using a pizza stone—or place the prebaked crust right on a pizza tray or a large baking sheet.

1. Heat the butter in a large skillet over medium heat. Add the garlic and cook for 1 minute.

2. Add the greens and cook, tossing often with tongs or two forks, until soft and wilted, about 4 minutes. Set aside.

3. Sprinkle the shredded mozzarella over the dough, leaving a ½-inch border around the edge.

4. Top with the greens mixture from the skillet, then sprinkle the blue cheese over the pizza. Grate the nutmeg over the top and sprinkle on the red pepper flakes, if desired.

5. Slip the pizza from the peel to the hot stone or place the pie on its tray or baking sheet either in the oven or on the unheated section of the grill. Bake or grill with the lid closed until the cheese has melted and is bubbling and the crust is firm to the touch, 16 to 18 minutes. Slip the peel back under the pie to take it off the hot stone, then set it aside—or transfer the pie on its tray or baking sheet to a wire rack. Cool for 5 minutes before slicing.

Chorizo and Red Pepper Pizza

This pie is a more sophisticated take on the pepperoni pie classic. Chorizo, a spicy pork sausage laced with smoked paprika, comes in two varieties: the traditional Spanish version, dried and ready to eat—and thus preferred here—and the Mexican version, which is raw and must be thinly sliced and fully cooked in a skillet with a little oil before being used on this pizza.

MAKES 1 PIZZA

Either all-purpose flour for dusting the peel or nonstick spray for greasing the pizza tray or a large baking sheet

One recipe homemade dough, preferably the Classic Pizza Dough (page 23); or 1 pound purchased fresh dough or frozen dough, thawed; or one 12- to 14-inch store-bought, prebaked plain pizza crust

1 medium red bell pepper

6 sun-dried tomatoes packed in oil

1 garlic clove, quartered

6 ounces mozzarella or Monterey Jack, shredded

4 ounces (¼ pound) ready-to-eat Spanish chorizo, thinly sliced

½ cup sliced pitted green olives

3 ounces Manchego or Parmigiano-Reggiano, shaved into thin strips

BAKING OPTIONS

With a pizza stone. Preheat the stone in the oven at 450°F for 30 to 45 minutes; or preheat the stone on a gas grill at medium, indirect heat (about 450°F) for 30 to 45 minutes; or build an indirect, medium-heat coal bed in a charcoal grill and preheat the stone for the same amount of time.

With a pizza tray or a large baking sheet. Preheat the oven to 450°F, a gas grill to indirect, medium heat (about 450°F), or build an indirect, medium-heat coal bed around the edge of a charcoal grill.

CRUST OPTIONS

Fresh dough on a pizza stone. Start out by dusting a pizza peel with flour, then set the dough at its center. Use your fingertips to dimple the dough, spreading it out a bit until it's a flattened circle. Pick it up and shape it by holding its edge and slowly turning it until it's about 14 inches in diameter. Set it floured side down on the peel.

Fresh dough on a baking sheet. Grease a pizza tray or a large baking sheet with non-stick spray. Lay the dough on the tray or baking sheet; dimple it with your finger-tips until it's a flattened circle—then pull and press it until it forms a 14-inch circle on the tray or an irregular 12 × 17-inch rectangle on the baking sheet.

A prebaked crust. Place it on a floured pizza peel if using a pizza stone—or place the prebaked crust right on a pizza tray or a large baking sheet.

1. If you have a gas cooktop, hold the pepper with a pair of flame-safe tongs over the open flame of one of the burners until blackened all over, turning often, about 5 minutes. Alternatively, place the pepper on a small, lipped baking sheet and broil 4 to 6 inches from a preheated broiler until blackened all around, turning occasion-ally, about 4 minutes. In either case, place the blackened pepper in a small bowl and seal tightly with plastic wrap; or seal in a paper bag. Set aside for 10 minutes. (See Note.)

2. Peel off the outer blackened bits from the pepper. There's no need to remove every little black bit. Stem, core, and seed the pepper before tearing it into large pieces.

3. Place these pieces in a food processor. Add the sun-dried tomatoes and garlic; process until a fairly smooth paste, scraping down the sides with a rubber spat-ula as necessary.

4. Spread the pepper mixture over the crust, leaving a ½-inch border at the edge. Top the pepper mixture with the shredded cheese, then arrange the chorizo slices over the pizza.

5. Sprinkle the olives over the pie, then lay the shaved strips of Manchego across the toppings.

6. Gently slip the pizza from the peel to the heated stone—or place the pie on the pizza tray or baking sheet either in the oven or over the unheated portion of the grill grate. Bake or grill with the lid closed until the cheese is bubbling and the crust has turned brown at its edges. If working with fresh dough, check it occasionally to pierce any air bubbles that may form, particularly at its edge and particularly during the first 10 minutes.

7. Slip the peel back under the pizza to get it off the stone for cooling—or transfer the pie on its tray or baking sheet to a wire rack. Cool for 5 minutes before slicing to serve. For a crisp crust, transfer the pizza from the peel, tray, or baking sheet right to the wire rack after a minute or two so the bottom doesn't steam and soften.

NOTE: Of course, you can forget all this fuss and simply use 1 whole jarred roasted red pepper or pimiento.

Delicata Squash and Chard Pizza

Delicata squash is a fall treat: a light, savory squash that takes far less time to cook than butternut or any winter squash. Plus, the skin is fully edible, an excellent source of fiber. To prepare it for cooking, cut the squash in half lengthwise, then scrape out the seeds and their sticky filaments with a serrated grapefruit spoon.

MAKES 1 PIZZA

All-purpose flour for the pizza peel or olive oil for the pizza tray or the baking sheet

One recipe homemade dough, preferably the Whole Wheat Pizza Dough (page 25); or 1 pound purchased fresh dough or frozen dough, thawed; or one 12- to 14-inch store-bought, prebaked plain pizza crust

1 tablespoon unsalted butter

1 small yellow onion, chopped (about ½ cup)

1 cup seeded and diced delicata squash (2 or 3 medium squash)

4 cups chopped, stemmed Swiss chard leaves

¼ cup dry white wine or dry vermouth

1 tablespoon maple syrup

1 teaspoon minced sage leaves or ½ teaspoon dried sage

½ teaspoon ground cinnamon

½ teaspoon salt

½ teaspoon freshly ground black pepper

8 ounces Fontina, shredded

BAKING OPTIONS

With a pizza stone. Position the rack in the middle of the oven and preheat the stone in the oven at 450°F for 30 to 45 minutes; or preheat the stone on a gas grill at medium, indirect heat (about 450°F) for 30 to 45 minutes; or build an

indirect, medium-heat coal bed in a charcoal grill and then preheat the stone for the same amount of time.

With a pizza tray or a large baking sheet. Preheat the oven to 450°F, a gas grill to indirect, medium heat (about 450°F), or build an indirect, medium-heat coal bed around the edge of a charcoal grill.

CRUST OPTIONS

Fresh dough on a pizza stone. Dust a pizza peel lightly with flour. Add the dough and form it into a large circle by dimpling it with your fingertips. Pick it up with both hands at its edge and rotate it slowly, letting gravity stretch the circle while you also do so at its edge, until it's about 14 inches in diameter. Set the shaped dough floured side down on the peel.

Fresh dough on a pizza tray or a large baking sheet. Grease the tray or baking sheet lightly with a little olive oil. Lay the dough at the center and dimple the dough with your fingertips to flatten it into a thick circle—then pull and press it until it forms a 14-inch circle on the tray or an irregular 12 × 7-inch rectangle on the baking sheet.

A prebaked crust. Place it on a floured pizza peel if using a pizza stone—or place the prebaked crust on a pizza tray or a large baking sheet.

1. Melt the butter in a large skillet set over medium heat; then add the onion and cook, stirring frequently, until translucent, about 3 minutes.

2. Stir in the diced squash and cook, stirring occasionally, for 4 minutes.

3. Add the chopped chard and pour in the wine or vermouth. Stir constantly until partially wilted; then stir in the maple syrup, sage, cinnamon, salt, and pepper.

4. Toss well, cover, reduce the heat to low, and cook, stirring occasionally, until the chard and squash are tender and the liquid has evaporated to a glaze, about 8 minutes.

5. Spread the shredded Fontina evenly over the crust, leaving a ½-inch border around its edge. Spoon the squash and chard topping evenly over the cheese.

6. Slip the crust off the peel and onto the heated stone or place the pie on its tray or baking sheet in the oven or over the unheated portion of the grill. Bake or grill with the lid closed until the cheese is bubbling and the crust has turned a golden brown, 16 to 18 minutes. Slip the peel back under the crust to remove it from the stone and cool for 5 minutes, or transfer the pie on its tray or baking sheet to a wire rack to cool for 5 minutes.

Duck Confit Pizza

This pizza is a riff on cassoulet, the French stew of white beans, sausage, and duck confit. Look for duck confit legs in the butcher case of some supermarkets or from online suppliers. And if you can't find smoked, ready-to-eat kielbasa, you'll need to fry the raw version with a little oil in a skillet over medium heat until cooked through.

MAKES 1 PIZZA

All-purpose flour for the pizza peel or nonstick spray for the pizza tray or the baking sheet

One recipe homemade dough, preferably the Classic Pizza Dough (page 23) or the Whole Wheat Pizza Dough (page 25); or 1 pound purchased fresh dough or frozen dough, thawed; or one 12- to 14-inch store-bought, prebaked plain pizza crust

4 ounces (¼ pound) Gruyère, shredded

⅔ cup canned white beans, drained and rinsed

1 head roasted garlic (see instructions in step 1 on page 105) or 12 roasted garlic cloves from the salad bar at the supermarket

2 tablespoons minced sage leaves or 1 tablespoon dried sage

2 teaspoons stemmed thyme leaves or 1 teaspoon dried thyme

½ teaspoon salt

½ teaspoon freshly ground black pepper

4 ounces duck confit legs, deboned and the meat shredded

3 ounces smoked, ready-to-eat kielbasa, thinly sliced

1½ ounces Parmigiano-Reggiano, finely grated

BAKING OPTIONS

With a pizza stone. Preheat the stone in the oven at 450°F for 30 to 45 minutes; or preheat the stone on a gas grill at medium, indirect heat (about 450°F) for 30

to 45 minutes; or build an indirect, medium-heat coal bed in a charcoal grill and preheat the stone for the same amount of time.

With a pizza tray or a baking sheet. Preheat the oven to 450°F, a gas grill to indirect, medium heat (about 450°F), or build an indirect, medium-heat coal bed around the edge of a charcoal grill.

CRUST OPTIONS

Fresh dough on a pizza stone. After you've dusted a pizza peel with flour, set the dough in its center and dimple the dough with your fingertips, stretching it out until it's a flattened, rippled circle. Pick it up by its edge and rotate it slowly in your hands, stretching the edge as you do so, until it's a circle about 14 inches in diameter. Set the dough floured side down on the peel.

Fresh dough on a pizza tray or a large baking sheet. Grease either with nonstick spray and set the dough in the center. Dimple the dough with your fingertips—then pull and press the dough until it forms a 14-inch circle on the tray or an irregular rectangle, about 12 inches long and 7 inches wide, on the baking sheet.

A prebaked crust. Place it on a floured pizza peel if using a pizza stone—or place the prebaked crust on a greased pizza tray or a large baking sheet.

1. Spread the shredded Gruyère over the crust, leaving a ½-inch border at the edge.

2. Top the cheese with the beans, then squeeze the garlic pulp out over the pizza. If you're using purchased roasted garlic, quarter the cloves so they can be sprinkled over the pie. Sprinkle with sage, thyme, salt, and pepper.

3. Arrange the shredded duck confit meat and the kielbasa rounds over the pie, then top with the grated Parmigiano-Reggiano. Slide the pie from the peel onto the heated stone or place the pie on its pizza tray or the baking sheet either in the oven or on the unheated portion of the grill's grate.

4. Bake or grill with the lid closed until the crust is lightly browned and somewhat firm to the touch, 16 to 18 minutes. If any air bubbles pop up around the edges of fresh dough, prick them with a fork. Slide the peel back under the pizza to remove it from the very hot stone—or transfer the pie on the pizza tray or the baking sheet to a wire rack. Cool for 5 minutes before slicing and serving. For an even crisper crust, take the pie off the peel, tray, or baking sheet after a minute or two and let it cool directly on the wire rack.

Meatball Pizza

Classic meatballs and tomato sauce top a pizza crust, along with some diced bell pepper and grated cheese.

MAKES 1 PIZZA

Either all-purpose flour for the pizza peel or olive oil for the pizza tray or the baking sheet

One recipe homemade dough, preferably the Classic Pizza Dough (page 23) or the Parmesan Pizza Dough (page 31); or 1 pound purchased fresh dough or frozen dough, thawed; or one 12-to 14-inch store-bought, prebaked plain pizza crust

8 ounces (½ pound) lean ground beef

¼ cup chopped parsley leaves

2 tablespoons plain dried bread crumbs

½ ounce Asiago, Grana Padano, or Pecorino, finely grated

2 teaspoons minced oregano leaves or 1 teaspoon dried oregano

½ teaspoon fennel seeds

¾ teaspoon salt

¾ teaspoon freshly ground black pepper

5 garlic cloves, minced

1 tablespoon olive oil

1 small yellow onion, chopped (about ½ cup)

One 14-ounce can crushed tomatoes

1 teaspoon stemmed thyme leaves or ½ teaspoon dried thyme

¼ teaspoon grated or ground nutmeg

¼ teaspoon ground cloves

¼ teaspoon red pepper flakes

6 ounces mozzarella, shredded

1 medium green bell pepper, cored, seeded, and diced

2 ounces Parmigiano-Reggiano, shaved into thin strips

BAKING OPTIONS

With a pizza stone. Preheat the stone in the oven at 450°F for 30 to 45 minutes; or preheat the stone on a gas grill at medium, indirect heat (about 450°F) for 30 to 45 minutes; or build an indirect, medium-heat coal bed in a charcoal grill and preheat the stone for the same amount of time.

With a pizza tray or a large baking sheet. Preheat the oven to 450°F, a gas grill to indirect, medium heat (about 450°F), or build an indirect, medium-heat coal bed around the edge of a charcoal grill.

CRUST OPTIONS

Fresh dough on a pizza stone. Dust a pizza peel with flour, place the dough at its center, and form the dough into a large circle by dimpling it with your fingertips. Pick it up and shape it by holding its edge and rotating it, all the while stretching it gently, until it's about 14 inches in diameter. Set it floured side down on the peel.

Fresh dough on a pizza tray or a large baking sheet. Dab a little olive oil on a paper towel and grease the tray or the baking sheet. Lay the dough in the middle and dimple the dough with your fingertips until it's a flattened circle—then pull and press it until it forms a 14-inch circle on the tray or an irregular 12 × 7-inch rectangle on the baking sheet.

A prebaked crust. Place it on a floured pizza peel if using a pizza stone—or place the prebaked crust on a greased pizza tray or a large baking sheet.

1. Mix the ground beef, parsley, bread crumbs, the grated cheese, oregano, fennel seeds, ½ teaspoon of the salt, ½ teaspoon of the pepper, and 1 minced garlic clove in a large bowl until well combined. Form into 10 meatballs, using about 2 tablespoons of the mixture for each one.

2. Heat the olive oil in a large saucepan over medium heat. Add the onion and the remaining 4 minced garlic cloves; cook, stirring often, until softened, about 3 minutes.

3. Stir in the crushed tomatoes, thyme, nutmeg, cloves, red pepper flakes, the remaining ¼ teaspoon salt, and the remaining ¼ teaspoon pepper. Add the meatballs and bring to a simmer.

4. Reduce the heat to low and simmer, uncovered, until the sauce has thickened and the meatballs are cooked through, about 20 minutes. Cool at room temperature for 20 minutes.

5. Spread the shredded mozzarella over the prepared crust, leaving a ½-inch border at the edge. Remove the meatballs from the tomato sauce and set them aside. Spoon and spread the tomato sauce over the cheese, taking care to keep the border intact.

6. Cut each meatball in half and place the halves cut side down all over the pie. Top with the diced bell pepper and then the shaved Parmigiano-Reggiano. Slip the pizza from the peel to the hot stone or place the pizza on its tray or baking sheet either in the oven or over the unheated portion of the grill grate.

7. Bake or grill with the lid closed until the sauce is bubbling and the crust has turned golden brown, 16 to 18 minutes. Slide the peel back under the crust to remove it from the hot stone or transfer the pie on the tray or the baking sheet to a wire rack. Cool for 5 minutes before slicing.

Mexican Shrimp Pizza

Think of this as a pizza version of shrimp nachos, with salsa as the pizza sauce. Want an easier version? Use 1 cup store-bought salsa, either jarred or fresh, found in the produce section or at the salad bar of most supermarkets. And buy 6 ounces precooked shrimp, usually available at the fish counter, if you don't have time to steam them yourself.

MAKES 1 PIZZA

All-purpose flour to dust the pizza peel or nonstick spray to grease the pizza
  tray or a large baking sheet
One recipe homemade dough, preferably the Classic Pizza Dough (page 23);
  or 1 pound purchased fresh dough or frozen dough, thawed; or one 12- to
  14-inch store-bought, prebaked plain pizza crust
6 ounces medium shrimp (about 30 per pound), peeled and deveined
8 ounces (½ pound) cherry tomatoes, minced (see Notes)
1 medium shallot, minced
1½ tablespoons minced cilantro leaves
1 tablespoon extra virgin olive oil
1 teaspoon red wine vinegar
¼ teaspoon salt
6 ounces Cheddar, shredded
1 medium jarred pickled jalapeño, seeded and minced
1 teaspoon cumin seeds, crushed (see Notes)

BAKING OPTIONS

With a pizza stone. Preheat the stone in the oven at 450°F for 30 to 45 minutes; or preheat the stone on a gas grill at medium, indirect heat (about 450°F) for 30 to 45 minutes; or build an indirect, medium-heat coal bed in a charcoal grill and preheat the stone for the same amount of time.

With a pizza tray or a large baking sheet. Preheat the oven to 450°F, a gas grill to indirect, medium heat (about 450°F), or build an indirect, medium-heat coal bed around the edge of a charcoal grill.

CRUST OPTIONS

Fresh dough on a pizza stone. Dust a pizza peel with flour, place the dough at its center, and form the dough into a large, flattened circle by dimpling it with your fingertips. Pick it up and shape it by holding its edge and slowly turning and stretching the dough until it's about 14 inches in diameter. Set it floured side down on the peel.

Fresh dough on a pizza tray or a large baking sheet. Grease either with nonstick spray, then set the dough at the center. Dimple the dough with your fingertips—then pull and press the dough until it forms a circle about 14 inches in diameter on the tray or an irregular 12 × 7-inch rectangle on the baking sheet.

A prebaked crust. Place it on a pizza peel if using a pizza stone—or place the prebaked crust right on a pizza tray or a large baking sheet.

1. Fit a medium saucepan with a vegetable steamer. Add an inch of water (but not so the water rides up into the steamer) to the pan and bring the water to a boil over high heat.

2. Add the shrimp, cover, reduce the heat to low, and steam until pink and firm, about 3 minutes. Remove and refresh under cool water to stop their cooking. Chop into bite-sized bits.

3. Mix the cherry tomatoes, shallot, cilantro, olive oil, vinegar, and salt in a small bowl. Spread this mixture over the prepared crust, leaving a ½-inch border at the rim.

4. Top with the shredded Cheddar, then sprinkle on the chopped shrimp, minced jalapeño, and the crushed cumin seeds. Slide the pizza from the peel to the hot stone or place the pie on its tray or baking sheet either in the oven or on the section of the grill grate that's not directly over the heat source or coals.

5. Bake or grill with the lid closed until the crust is golden and the cheese has melted, 16 to 18 minutes. If working with fresh dough, whether homemade or store-bought, check it occasionally so you can prick any air bubbles that may arise on its surface. When the pizza's done, slip the peel back under it to get it off the stone or transfer the pie on its tray or baking sheet to a wire rack. Cool for 5 minutes before slicing and serving.

NOTES: To mince tomatoes (or most vegetables), cut them into chunks, place them on a cutting board, and rock a large chef's knife through them, seesawing the blade by its handle, using the other end as the pivot point in the seesaw action. Crush the cumin seeds in a mortar with a pestle or seal them in a small zip-closed plastic bag and crush them with the bottom of a heavy saucepan against a cutting board.

Nacho Pizza

Forget the chips; the pizza crust is a fine stand-in for them. While we prefer this pie with green salsa made from chiles and tomatillos, you can use any kind you like, from a fruit-and-chile in the bottle to a good, hearty tomato salsa.

MAKES 1 PIZZA

Yellow cornmeal for dusting the pizza peel or nonstick spray for greasing the pizza tray or a large baking sheet

One recipe homemade dough, preferably the Classic Pizza Dough (page 23); or 1 pound purchased fresh dough or frozen dough, thawed; or one 12- to 14-inch store-bought, prebaked plain pizza crust

1¼ cups canned refried beans

6 ounces Monterey Jack, shredded

3 medium plum tomatoes, chopped

½ teaspoon ground cumin

1 teaspoon minced oregano leaves or ½ teaspoon dried oregano

½ teaspoon salt

½ teaspoon freshly ground black pepper

⅔ cup salsa, preferably a green (or "verde") salsa

½ cup regular or low-fat sour cream (do not use fat-free, which can break when set over a hot pizza)

Jarred pickled jalapeño slices, to taste

BAKING OPTIONS

With a pizza stone. Preheat the stone in the oven at 450°F for 30 to 45 minutes; or preheat the stone on a gas grill at medium, indirect heat (about 450°F) for 30 to 45 minutes; or build an indirect, medium-heat coal bed in a charcoal grill and preheat the stone for the same amount of time.

With a pizza tray or a large baking sheet. Preheat the oven to 450°F, a gas grill to indirect, medium heat (about 450°F), or build an indirect, medium-heat coal bed around the edge of a charcoal grill.

CRUST OPTIONS

Fresh dough on a pizza stone. Dust a pizza peel with cornmeal, place the dough at its center, and form the dough into a large circle by dimpling it with your fingertips. Pick it up and shape it with your hands at its edge, slowly turning the dough until it's about 14 inches in diameter. Set it cornmeal side down on the peel.

Fresh dough on a pizza tray or a large baking sheet. Grease the tray or baking sheet with nonstick spray. Lay the dough at the center and dimple the dough with your fingertips until it's a large, flattened circle—then pull and press it until it forms a 14-inch circle on the tray or an irregular rectangle, about 12×7 inches, on the baking sheet.

A prebaked crust. Place it on a pizza peel if using a pizza stone—or place the prebaked crust right on a pizza tray or a large baking sheet.

1. Use a rubber spatula to spread the refried beans over the crust, evenly coating it but leaving a ½-inch border at the edge. Top the beans with the shredded Monterey Jack.

2. Stir the chopped tomatoes, cumin, oregano, salt, and pepper in a large bowl, then spread evenly over the cheese. Dot the salsa in small spoonfuls over the crust.

3. Slip the pizza from the peel to the heated stone or place the pie on its tray or baking sheet in the oven or on the grill grate over indirect heat. Bake or grill with the lid closed until the cheese is bubbling and the beans are hot, 16 to 18 minutes.

4. Slip the peel back under the crust and set aside or transfer the pie on the tray or baking sheet to a wire rack. Cool for 5 minutes. For a crisper crust, remove the pizza from the peel, tray, or baking sheet after a minute or two to let it cool directly on the wire rack.

5. Top the pie with dabs of sour cream and as many jalapeño slices as you like before slicing and serving.

Peas and Carrots Pizza

This classic side dish can now be a classic pizza, complete with a creamy white sauce, reminiscent of the filling in many pot pies.

MAKES 1 PIZZA

All-purpose flour for the pizza peel or nonstick spray for the pizza tray or a large baking sheet

One recipe homemade dough, preferably the Whole Wheat Pizza Dough (page 25); or 1 pound purchased fresh dough or frozen dough, thawed; or one 12- to 14-inch store-bought, prebaked plain pizza crust

2 tablespoons unsalted butter

1½ tablespoons all-purpose flour

½ cup whole, low-fat, or fat-free milk

½ cup heavy, whipping, or light cream

3 ounces Swiss or Emmental, shredded

2 teaspoons stemmed thyme leaves or 1 teaspoon dried thyme

½ teaspoon grated nutmeg

1 cup fresh shelled peas or frozen peas, thawed

1 cup diced carrots (if using frozen, then thawed)

3 garlic cloves, minced

1 ounce Parmigiano-Reggiano, finely grated

BAKING OPTIONS

With a pizza stone. Preheat the stone in the oven at 450°F for 30 to 45 minutes; or preheat the stone on a gas grill at medium, indirect heat (about 450°F) for 30 to 45 minutes; or build an indirect, medium-heat coal bed in a charcoal grill and preheat the stone for the same amount of time.

With a pizza tray or a large baking sheet. Preheat the oven to 450°F, a gas grill to indirect, medium heat (about 450°F), or build an indirect, medium-heat fire around the edge of a charcoal grill.

CRUST OPTIONS

Fresh dough on a pizza stone. Dust a pizza peel with flour, set the dough at its center, and dimple the dough into a flattened, large circle with your fingertips. Pick it up and shape it by holding its edge, rotating it slowly and gently stretching the dough until the circle is about 14 inches in diameter. Set the dough floured side down on the peel.

Fresh dough on a pizza tray or a large baking sheet. Grease either with nonstick spray; set the dough at the center of either. Dimple the dough with your fingertips until it's a flattened, squashed circle—then pull and press it until it forms a 14-inch circle on the tray or a 12×7-inch irregular rectangle on the baking sheet.

A prebaked crust. Place it on a floured pizza peel if using a pizza stone—or place the prebaked crust right on a pizza tray or a large baking sheet.

1. Melt the butter in a large skillet set over medium heat. Whisk in the flour and continue whisking until smooth and very light beige.

2. Whisk in the milk in a slow, steady stream; then whisk in the cream. Continue whisking over the heat until thick, about like fairly thin melted ice cream. Stir in the shredded cheese, thyme, and nutmeg until smooth. Cool at room temperature for 10 minutes.

3. Meanwhile, slip the untopped crust from the peel to the heated stone or place the crust on its tray or the baking sheet either in the oven or over the unheated portion of the grill grate. Bake or grill with the lid closed until the crust just begins to feel firm at its edges and just begins to brown, about 10 minutes. If you're using fresh dough, you'll need to pop any air bubbles that may arise over its surface or at its edges as it bakes. Slide the peel back under the partially baked crust and remove it from the oven or grill—or else transfer the crust on the tray or baking sheet to a wire rack.

4. Spread the thickened milk-based sauce over the crust, leaving a $\frac{1}{2}$-inch border at the edge. Top the sauce with the peas and carrots, then sprinkle the garlic evenly over the pie. Finally, sprinkle the grated Parmigiano-Reggiano over the toppings.

5. Return the pizza to the oven or grill, either back onto the heated stone or on its tray or baking sheet (again, over the unheated portion of the grill grate). Continue baking until the cheese and sauce are bubbling and the crust is golden brown, about 12 minutes. Once again slide the peel under the crust to remove it from the stone or place the pie on its tray or baking sheet back over the wire rack. Set aside to cool for 5 minutes before slicing.

Philly Cheesesteak Pizza

In Philadelphia, the cheesesteak sandwich is comfort food deluxe: strips of meat topped with a cheesy sauce, all served on a hoagie bun—or here, on a newfangled pie. Look for rare roast beef at the deli counter of most high-end markets; have it sliced paper thin to top this hearty pie.

MAKES 1 PIZZA

All-purpose flour for the pizza peel or nonstick spray for the pizza tray or a
   large baking sheet
One recipe homemade dough, preferably the Classic Pizza Dough (page 23);
   or 1 pound purchased fresh dough or frozen dough, thawed; or one 12- to
   14-inch store-bought, prebaked plain pizza crust
1 tablespoon unsalted butter
1 small yellow onion, halved through its stem and thinly sliced
1 small green bell pepper, seeded and very thinly sliced (see Note)
2 tablespoons Worcestershire sauce
Several dashes hot red pepper sauce
6 tablespoons Classic Pizza Sauce (page 38), No-Cook Pizza Sauce
   (page 39), or jarred plain pizza sauce
8 ounces (½ pound) mozzarella, shredded
6 ounces deli roast beef, shaved paper thin and cut into strips
3 ounces provolone, shredded

BAKING OPTIONS

With a pizza stone. Preheat the stone in the oven at 450°F for 30 to 45 minutes; or preheat the stone on a gas grill at medium, indirect heat (about 450°F) for 30 to 45 minutes; or build an indirect, medium-heat coal bed in a charcoal grill and preheat the stone for the same amount of time.

With a pizza tray or a large baking sheet. Preheat the oven to 450°F, a gas grill to indirect, medium heat (about 450°F), or build an indirect, medium-heat coal bed around the edge of a charcoal grill.

CRUST OPTIONS

Fresh dough on a pizza stone. Dust a pizza peel lightly with flour. Add the dough and form it into a large circle by dimpling it with your fingertips. Pick it up by its edge and shape it by slowly turning it and gently stretching it until it's about 14 inches in diameter. Set it floured side down on the peel.

Fresh dough on a pizza tray or a large baking sheet. Grease the tray or baking sheet with nonstick spray. Lay the dough at the center and dimple it with your fingertips until it's a squashed circle—then pull and press the dough until it forms a circle about 14 inches in diameter on the tray or an irregular rectangle, about 12 × 7 inches, on the baking sheet.

A prebaked crust. Place it on a floured pizza peel if using a pizza stone—or place the prebaked crust on a pizza tray or a large baking sheet.

1. Melt the butter in a large skillet set over medium heat. Add the onion and bell pepper; cook, stirring often, until softened, about 5 minutes.

2. Stir in the Worcestershire sauce and the hot red pepper sauce (to taste). Continue cooking until the liquid in the skillet has reduced to a glaze, about 2 more minutes. Cool at room temperature for 5 minutes.

3. Use a rubber spatula to spread the pizza sauce over the prepared crust, leaving a ½-inch border at the edge. Top with the shredded mozzarella.

4. Lay the roast beef strips evenly over the pie, then spoon and spread the vegetable mixture over the beef. Top with the shredded provolone.

5. Slip the pizza from the peel to the hot stone or place the pizza on its tray or baking sheet either in the oven or over the part of the grill grate that's not right over the heat source. Bake or grill with the lid closed until the crust is golden, evenly browned on its underside, and the cheese has melted and even begun to turn a very light brown, about 18 minutes. Once or twice, check fresh dough, whether homemade or store-bought, to prick any air bubbles that may arise on its surface, particularly at the edge.

6. Once the pie is done, slide the peel back under it to take it off the hot stone or transfer the pie on its tray or baking sheet to a wire rack. Cool for 5 minutes before slicing and serving. If you want to make sure the crust stays crisp, transfer the hot pie from the peel, tray, or baking sheet right onto the wire rack after a minute or two.

NOTE: You can also add 8 ounces sliced mushrooms to the onion and bell pepper in the sauté. You'll need to let the mixture cook an extra 3 or 4 minutes after you add the Worcestershire sauce, just to make sure the mushrooms release most of their moisture and it evaporates to a glaze.

Polynesian Pizza

Salty ham and sweet pineapple are a classic combo on a pie—and even better if you use chewy Canadian bacon (actually smoked pork loin) and fresh cubed pineapple (available in containers in the produce section of most supermarkets). A few sesame seeds and some Indonesian soy sauce add a sophisticated touch.

MAKES 1 PIZZA

All-purpose flour to dust the pizza peel or nonstick spray to grease the pizza tray or a large baking sheet

One recipe homemade dough, preferably the Classic Pizza Dough (page 23); or 1 pound purchased fresh dough or frozen dough, thawed; or one 12- to 14-inch store-bought, prebaked plain pizza crust

3 tablespoons kecap manis or sweet thick Indonesian soy sauce (see Note)

6 ounces mozzarella, shredded

3 ounces Canadian bacon, diced

1 cup fresh pineapple chunks

½ cup thinly sliced scallions

1 tablespoon sesame seeds

BAKING OPTIONS

With a pizza stone. Preheat the stone in the oven at 450°F for 30 to 45 minutes; or preheat the stone on a gas grill at medium, indirect heat (about 450°F) for 30 to 45 minutes; or build an indirect, medium-heat coal bed in a charcoal grill and preheat the stone for the same amount of time.

With a pizza tray or a large baking sheet. Preheat the oven to 450°F, a gas grill to indirect, medium heat (about 450°F), or build an indirect, medium-heat coal bed around the edge of a charcoal grill.

CRUST OPTIONS

Fresh dough on a pizza stone. Dust a pizza peel with flour, set the dough at its center, and form the dough into a large, flattened circle by dimpling it with your fingertips. Pick it up by the edge and stretch it by rotating it until it's about 14 inches in diameter. Set the shaped dough floured side down on the peel.

Fresh dough on a pizza tray or a large baking sheet. Grease the tray or baking sheet with nonstick spray. Lay the dough at the center of either and dimple the dough with your fingertips—then pull and press it until it forms a 14-inch circle on the tray or an irregular 12 × 7-inch rectangle on the baking sheet.

A prebaked crust. Place it on a floured pizza peel if using a pizza stone—or place the prebaked crust on a pizza tray or a large baking sheet.

1. Spread the kecap manis evenly over the dough, leaving a ½-inch border at the edge. Sprinkle the shredded mozzarella evenly over the sauce.

2. Top the pizza with the Canadian bacon, pineapple chunks, and sliced scallions—then sprinkle the sesame seeds evenly over the pie.

3. Slip the crust from the peel to the very hot stone or place the pie on its tray or baking sheet in the oven or on the grill over the unheated portion. Bake or grill with the lid closed until the cheese has melted and the crust is golden brown, 16 to 18 minutes.

4. Slip the peel back under the crust to remove it from the hot stone or transfer the pie on its tray or baking sheet to a wire rack. Cool the pizza on the peel or the baking rack for 5 minutes before slicing. To ensure that the crust stays crunchy, transfer the pizza from the peel, tray, or baking sheet right to the wire rack after a minute or so.

NOTE: Kecap manis [pronounced KEH-chuhp MAH-nees] is an Indonesian condiment, rather like soy sauce but thicker, less salty, sweetened with palm sugar, and flavored with garlic and star anise. Look for it at Asian markets and from suppliers on the Web. For a less interesting substitute, use hoisin sauce or oyster sauce.

Pot Pie Pizza

Think of this pizza as an upside-down pot pie: the crust on the bottom, the creamy filling on top. Use the meat from a rotisserie chicken, or buy fresh-roasted turkey or chicken breast at the deli counter. Have it sliced into thick slabs so you can cut it into chunks at home.

MAKES 1 PIZZA

Yellow cornmeal for the pizza peel or nonstick spray for the pizza tray or a
  large baking sheet
One recipe homemade dough, preferably the Classic Pizza Dough (page 23);
  or 1 pound purchased fresh dough or frozen dough, thawed; or one 12- to
  14-inch store-bought, prebaked plain pizza crust
1 tablespoon unsalted butter
1½ tablespoons all-purpose flour
1 cup whole, low-fat, or fat-free milk, at room temperature
1 tablespoon Dijon mustard
1½ teaspoons stemmed thyme leaves or 1 teaspoon dried thyme
1 teaspoon minced sage leaves or ½ teaspoon dried sage
1 cup chopped, skinned, deboned, cooked chicken or turkey meat
2 cups frozen mixed vegetables, thawed
2 teaspoons Worcestershire sauce
½ teaspoon salt
½ teaspoon freshly ground black pepper
Several dashes hot red pepper sauce
6 ounces Gouda, Emmental, Swiss, or Cheddar, shredded

BAKING OPTIONS

With a pizza stone. Position the rack in the middle of the oven and preheat the stone in the oven at 450°F for 30 to 45 minutes; or preheat the stone on a gas grill at medium, indirect heat (about 450°F) for 30 to 45 minutes; or build an

indirect, medium-heat coal bed in a charcoal grill and then preheat the stone for the same amount of time.

With a pizza tray or a large baking sheet. Preheat the oven to 450°F, a gas grill to indirect, medium heat (about 450°F), or build an indirect, medium-heat coal bed around the edge of a charcoal grill.

CRUST OPTIONS

Fresh dough on a pizza stone. Start out by dusting a pizza peel with cornmeal, then set the dough at its center. Dimple the dough with your fingertips into a large, flattened circle—then pick it up, hold it by its edge, and rotate it in front of you, all the while gently stretching it until it's about 14 inches in diameter. Set the shaped dough cornmeal side down on the peel.

Fresh dough on a pizza tray or a large baking sheet. Grease one or the other with nonstick spray. Lay the dough at the center of either and dimple the dough with your fingertips—then pull and press it until it forms a circle about 14 inches in diameter on the tray or a 12 × 7-inch irregular rectangle on the baking sheet.

A prebaked crust. Place it on a cornmeal-dusted pizza peel if using a pizza stone—or place the prebaked crust right on a pizza tray or a large baking sheet.

1. Melt the butter in a large saucepan over medium heat. Whisk in the flour until fairly smooth, then continue whisking over the heat until light blond, about 30 seconds.

2. Whisk in the milk in a slow, steady stream. Continue whisking over the heat until thickened, about like melted ice cream. Whisk in the mustard and herbs.

3. Remove the pan from the heat and stir in the meat and vegetables; then stir in the Worcestershire sauce, salt, pepper, and hot red pepper sauce (to taste).

Stir in the shredded cheese until everything is uniform and coated in the sauce. Spread evenly over the crust, leaving a ½-inch border at the edge.

4. Slip the crust off the peel and onto the stone, or place the pie on its tray or baking sheet in the oven or over the unheated section of the grill. Bake or grill with the lid closed until the filling is bubbling and the crust has turned a golden brown and is somewhat firm to the touch, about 18 minutes. Check on a fresh-dough pie occasionally to make sure there are no air bubbles in the crust; pop any that form.

5. Slip the peel back under the crust to remove the pie from the stone or transfer the pie on its tray or baking sheet to a wire rack. Set aside to cool for 5 minutes before slicing. If desired, transfer the pie directly to the wire rack after a minute or so to let the crust cool a bit without resting against another hot surface.

Potato, Onion, and Chutney Pizza

Potatoes on pizza? Indeed. They add a subtle richness to a pie, especially when they're set off with tangy chutney and a sliced sweet onion. Don't use russets or other baking potatoes here; instead, use white boiling potatoes that will turn creamy (rather than starchy) when steamed.

MAKES 1 PIZZA

All-purpose flour to dust the pizza peel or nonstick spray to grease the pizza tray or a large baking sheet

One recipe homemade dough, preferably the Classic Pizza Dough (page 23); or 1 pound purchased fresh dough or frozen dough, thawed; or one 12- to 14-inch store-bought, prebaked plain pizza crust

12 ounces (¾ pound) white boiling potatoes, such as Irish cobblers, peeled

6 tablespoons mango chutney, blueberry chutney, or another fruit-based chutney

6 ounces Monterey Jack, grated

3 tablespoons minced dill fronds or 1 tablespoon dried dill

1 large sweet onion, such as a Vidalia

BAKING OPTIONS

With a pizza stone. Preheat the stone in the oven at 450°F for 30 to 45 minutes; or preheat the stone on a gas grill at medium, indirect heat (about 450°F) for 30 to 45 minutes; or build an indirect, medium-heat coal bed in a charcoal grill and preheat the stone for the same amount of time.

With a pizza tray or a large baking sheet. Preheat the oven to 450°F, a gas grill to indirect, medium heat (about 450°F), or build an indirect, medium-heat coal bed around the edge of a charcoal grill.

CRUST OPTIONS

Fresh dough on a pizza stone. Dust a pizza peel lightly with flour. Add the dough and form it into a large circle by dimpling it with your fingertips. Pick it up, hold its edge, and slowly rotate it, stretching it all the while, until it's about 14 inches in diameter. Set the dough floured side down on the peel.

Fresh dough on a pizza tray or a large baking sheet. Grease the tray or baking sheet with nonstick spray. Lay the dough at the center of either; dimple the dough with your fingertips until it's a thick, flattened circle—then pull and press the dough until it forms a 14-inch circle on the tray or an irregular 12 × 7-inch rectangle on the baking sheet.

A prebaked crust. Place it on a pizza peel if using a pizza stone—or place the prebaked crust on a pizza tray or a large baking sheet.

1. While the oven or grill heats, bring about 1 inch water to a boil in a large saucepan fitted with a vegetable steamer. Add the potatoes, cover, reduce the heat to medium, and steam until tender when pierced with a fork, about 10 minutes. Transfer to a colander set in the sink and cool for 5 minutes, then slice into very thin rounds.

2. Spread the chutney evenly over the prepared crust, leaving about a ½-inch border at the edge. Top evenly with the grated Monterey Jack.

3. Arrange the potato slices evenly and decoratively over the pie, then sprinkle with the dill.

4. Slice the onion in half through its stem. Set it cut side down on your cutting board and use a very sharp knife to make paper-thin slices. Separate these slices into their individual strips and lay these over the pie.

5. Slide the pie from the peel to the very hot stone, taking care to keep the toppings in place; or place the pie on its tray or baking sheet either in the oven or on the section of the grill's grate that's not directly over the heat source. Bake or grill with the lid closed until the crust is lightly browned at its edge, even more darkly browned on its underside, 16 to 18 minutes. If any air bubbles arise at the edge or in the middle of fresh dough, pop them with a fork to produce an even crust. Slip the peel back under the hot pie on the stone or transfer the pie on its tray or baking sheet to a wire rack. Set aside to cool for 5 minutes before slicing and serving. Transfer the pizza from the peel, tray, or baking sheet right to the wire rack after a minute or so to make sure the crust stays crunchy on the bottom.

Prosciutto and Arugula Pizza

Unlike the Steak and Arugula Pizza (page 131), this is not a salad pie—that is, it's not a baked pie topped with a dressed salad. Rather, the arugula is baked with the cheese to create a peppery bite under the prosciutto.

MAKES 1 PIZZA

All-purpose flour for the pizza peel or olive oil for the pizza tray or the baking sheet

One recipe homemade dough, preferably the Semolina Pizza Dough (page 29); or 1 pound purchased fresh dough or frozen dough, thawed; or one 12- to 14-inch store-bought, prebaked plain pizza crust

¼ cup Classic Pizza Sauce (page 38), No-Cook Pizza Sauce (page 39), or jarred plain pizza sauce

3 ounces fresh mozzarella, thinly sliced

½ cup packed arugula leaves, thick stems removed

2 ounces prosciutto, shaved into thin strips

1 tablespoon balsamic vinegar

BAKING OPTIONS

With a pizza stone. Preheat the stone in the oven at 450°F for 30 to 45 minutes; or preheat the stone on a gas grill at medium, indirect heat (about 450°F) for 30 to 45 minutes; or build an indirect, medium-heat coal bed in a charcoal grill and preheat the stone for the same amount of time.

With a pizza tray or a large baking sheet. Preheat the oven to 450°F, a gas grill to indirect, medium heat (about 450°F), or build an indirect, medium-heat fire around the edge of a charcoal grill.

CRUST OPTIONS

Fresh dough on a pizza stone. Dust a pizza peel with flour, set the dough at its center, and dimple the dough into a large, flattened circle with your fingertips. Pick it up and shape it with your hands, holding the edge, slowly turning it and stretching it until it's about 14 inches in diameter. Set the shaped dough floured side down on the peel.

Fresh dough on a pizza tray or a large baking sheet. Grease either lightly with some olive oil dabbed on a paper towel. Lay the dough on the tray or baking sheet; dimple the dough with your fingertips—then pull and press it until it forms a 14-inch circle on the tray or a 12 × 7-inch rather irregular rectangle on the baking sheet.

A prebaked crust. Place it on a floured pizza peel if using a pizza stone—or place the prebaked crust on a pizza tray or a large baking sheet.

1. Spread the pizza sauce evenly over the crust, leaving a ½-inch border at the edge.

2. Arrange the mozzarella slices evenly over the pie, keeping that border clean.

3. Lay the arugula leaves over the pie, then top with the prosciutto strips. Slip the pizza from the peel to the hot stone or place the pie on its tray or baking sheet with the pizza either in the oven or on the section of the grill grate that's not directly over the heat source.

4. Bake or grill with the lid closed until the crust is golden as well as somewhat firm and the cheese has melted, 14 to 16 minutes. If working with fresh dough, check it during the first 10 minutes so you can pop any bubbles that may arise, particularly at the edge. Slip the peel back under the hot pie to take it off the stone or transfer the pie on its tray or baking sheet to a wire rack. Drizzle the pie with the balsamic vinegar, then set aside to cool for 5 minutes before slicing.

Reuben Pizza

L ike the deli sandwich on which it is modeled, this pizza is only as good as the corned beef and sauerkraut you use.

MAKES 1 PIZZA

Either all-purpose flour for the peel or nonstick spray for the pizza tray or baking sheet

One recipe homemade dough, preferably the Classic Pizza Dough (page 23); or 1 pound purchased fresh dough or frozen dough, thawed; or one 12- to 14-inch store-bought, prebaked plain pizza crust

3 tablespoons deli mustard

1 cup drained sauerkraut, squeezed in batches over the sink to remove excess moisture (see Note)

6 ounces Swiss, Emmental, Jarlsberg, or Jarlsberg Light, shredded

4 ounces (¼ pound) cooked deli corned beef, cut into thick slices and chopped

BAKING OPTIONS

With a pizza stone. Preheat the stone in the oven at 450°F for 30 to 45 minutes; or preheat the stone on a gas grill at medium, indirect heat (about 450°F) for 30 to 45 minutes; or build an indirect, medium-heat coal bed in a charcoal grill and preheat the stone for the same amount of time.

With a pizza tray or a large baking sheet. Preheat the oven to 450°F, a gas grill to indirect, medium heat (about 450°F), or build an indirect, medium-heat coal bed around the edge of a charcoal grill.

CRUST OPTIONS

Fresh dough on a pizza stone. Dust a pizza peel with flour; set the dough at its center. Form the dough into a large circle by dimpling it with your fingertips.

Pick it up and shape it with your hands, holding its edge, slowly turning the dough and gently stretching its edge until it's about 14 inches in diameter. Set it floured side down on the peel.

Fresh dough on a pizza tray or a large baking sheet. Grease either one with non-stick spray. Lay the dough at the center of either and dimple the dough with your fingertips until it's a thick, flattened circle—then pull and press the dough until it forms a 14-inch circle on the pizza tray or an irregular 12×7-inch rectangle on the baking sheet.

A prebaked crust. Place it on a pizza peel if using a pizza stone—or place the prebaked crust right on a pizza tray or a large baking sheet.

1. Spread the mustard evenly over the prepared crust, leaving a ½-inch border at the edge. Spread the sauerkraut evenly over the mustard.

2. Top the pie with the shredded cheese, then the chopped corned beef. Carefully slide the pizza from the peel to the heated stone or place the pie on its tray or baking sheet in the oven or over the portion of the grill grate not directly over the heat or coals.

3. Bake or grill with the lid closed until the crust has firmed up and turned golden and until the cheese has melted and browned a little, 16 to 18 minutes. If any air bubbles arise on fresh dough, particularly at its edge, pop them for an even crust. Slip the peel back under the pizza, taking care not to dislodge the topping, to remove the pie from the hot stone or transfer the pie on its tray or baking sheet to a wire rack. Set aside to cool for 5 minutes before slicing and serving.

NOTE: The best sauerkraut is found in sealed plastic packs at the deli case of most supermarkets.

Roasted Roots Pizza

Root vegetables are here first roasted to soften and sweeten them. While the recipe calls for half a sweet potato and the like—because that's enough for one pie—consider making two pies, doubling the recipe, rather than using half-portions of the various vegetables. Note that the oven or grill temperature starts slightly lower than usual to roast the vegetables, then it's increased to 450°F to grill or bake the pie.

MAKES 1 PIZZA

All-purpose flour for dusting the pizza peel or olive oil for greasing the pizza tray or the baking sheet

One recipe homemade dough, preferably the Whole Wheat Pizza Dough (page 25); or 1 pound purchased fresh dough or frozen dough, thawed; or one 12- to 14-inch store-bought, prebaked plain pizza crust

½ large garlic head (about 8 cloves, unpeeled)

½ small sweet potato, peeled, halved lengthwise, and thinly sliced

½ small fennel bulb, halved, trimmed, and thinly sliced

½ small parsnip, peeled, halved lengthwise, and thinly sliced

1 tablespoon olive oil

½ teaspoon salt

4 ounces (¼ pound) mozzarella, shredded

1 ounce Parmigiano-Reggiano, finely grated

1 tablespoon syrupy balsamic vinegar

BAKING OPTIONS

With a pizza stone. Preheat the stone in the oven at 400°F for 30 to 45 minutes; or preheat the stone on a gas grill at medium, indirect heat (about 400°F) for 30 to 45 minutes; or build an indirect, medium-heat coal bed in a charcoal grill and preheat the stone for the same amount of time.

With a pizza tray or a large baking sheet. Preheat the oven to 400°F, a gas grill to indirect, medium heat (about 400°F), or build an indirect, medium-heat coal bed around the edge of a charcoal grill.

CRUST OPTIONS

Fresh dough on a pizza stone. Dust a pizza peel lightly with flour. Add the dough and form it into a large circle by dimpling it with your fingertips. Pick it up, hold it by its edge with both hands, and slowly rotate it, stretching the edge a little each time, until the circle is about 14 inches in diameter. Set floured side down on the peel.

Fresh dough on a pizza tray or a large baking sheet. Grease the tray or baking sheet with some olive oil dabbed on a paper towel. Lay the dough at the center of either; dimple the dough with your fingertips—then pull and press it until it forms a 14-inch circle on the tray or an irregular rectangle, about 12 × 7 inches, on the baking sheet.

A prebaked crust. Place it on a floured pizza peel if using a pizza stone—or place the prebaked crust right on a pizza tray or a large baking sheet.

1. Wrap the unpeeled garlic cloves in a small aluminum foil packet and bake or grill directly over the heat for 40 minutes.

2. Meanwhile, toss the sweet potato, fennel, and parsnip in a large bowl with the olive oil and salt. Pour the contents of the bowl onto a large baking sheet. Place in the oven or over the unheated section of the grill and roast, turning occasionally, until soft and sweet, 15 to 20 minutes.

3. Transfer the garlic to a cutting board; open the packet, taking care to mind the steam. Also set the baking sheet with the vegetables aside on a wire rack.

4. Increase the oven's or gas grill's temperature to 450°F, or add a few more coals to the charcoal grill to raise the heat slightly.

5. Spread the shredded mozzarella over the prepared crust, leaving a ½-inch border at the edge. Top the cheese with all the vegetables; squeeze the pulpy, soft garlic out of its papery hulls and onto the pie. Top with the grated Parmigiano-Reggiano.

6. Slide the pizza from the peel to the hot stone or place the pizza on its tray or baking sheet either in the oven or over the unheated section of the grill. Bake or grill with the lid closed until the crust has turned golden brown and even darkened a bit on its bottom, until the cheese has melted and started to brown, 16 to 18 minutes. Fresh dough may develop some air bubbles during the first 10 minutes, particularly at its edge; pop these with a fork to assure an even crust.

7. Slide the peel back under the crust to take it off the hot stone or transfer the pizza on its tray or baking sheet to a wire rack. Set aside for 5 minutes. To keep the crust crunchy, you might want to transfer the pie from the peel, tray, or baking sheet right onto the wire rack to cool after a minute or so. Once cooled a bit, drizzle the pie with the balsamic vinegar, then slice into wedges to serve.

Sausage and Apple Pizza

Sausages and apples are a favorite German combination, so they make a dual appearance here on this savory pie. Since pork sausage can be rather heavy, this pie is best with chicken or turkey sausage, a little lighter contrast with the sweet/tart apple.

MAKES 1 PIZZA

Yellow cornmeal to dust the pizza peel or nonstick spray to grease the pizza tray or a large baking sheet

One recipe homemade dough, preferably the Classic Pizza Dough (page 23); or 1 pound purchased fresh dough or frozen dough, thawed; or one 12- to 14-inch store-bought, prebaked plain pizza crust

1 tablespoon olive oil

8 ounces (½ pound) chicken or turkey sausage

1 tablespoon coarse-ground mustard

6 ounces Fontina, shredded

1 small green apple, preferably a tart apple like a Granny Smith, peeled, cored, and thinly sliced

2 tablespoons chopped rosemary leaves, or parsley leaves, or stemmed thyme leaves, or a combination of any two to equal 2 tablespoons

1½ ounces Parmigiano-Reggiano, Pecorino, or Grana Padano, finely grated

BAKING OPTIONS

With a pizza stone. Preheat the stone in the oven at 450°F for 30 to 45 minutes; or preheat the stone on a gas grill at medium, indirect heat (about 450°F) for 30 to 45 minutes; or build an indirect, medium-heat coal bed in a charcoal grill and preheat the stone for the same amount of time.

With a pizza tray or a large baking sheet. Preheat the oven to 450°F, a gas grill to indirect, medium heat (about 450°F), or build an indirect, medium-heat coal bed around the edge of a charcoal grill.

CRUST OPTIONS

Fresh dough on a pizza stone. Dust a pizza peel lightly with cornmeal. Add the dough and form it into a large circle by dimpling it with your fingertips. Pick it up and shape it by holding its edge in both hands, rotating it slowly, and stretching it gently all the while, until the circle is about 14 inches in diameter. Set the dough cornmeal side down on the peel.

Fresh dough on a pizza tray or a large baking sheet. Grease one or the other with nonstick spray. Lay the dough at the center of either; dimple the dough with your fingertips until it's a thick, flat circle. Then pull and press it until it forms a 14-inch circle on the tray or a 12 × 7-inch irregular rectangle on the baking sheet.

A prebaked crust. Place it on a cornmeal-dusted pizza peel if using a pizza stone—or place the prebaked crust on a pizza tray or a large baking sheet.

1. Heat a large skillet over medium heat. Swirl in the olive oil, then add the sausage. Cook, turning occasionally, until well browned on all sides and cooked through. Transfer to a cutting board and slice into thin rounds.

2. Spread the mustard evenly over the prepared crust, leaving a ½-inch border at the edge. Top with the shredded Fontina, then lay the sliced sausage evenly over the pie.

3. Tuck the apple slices among the sausage rounds, then sprinkle with one of the chopped herbs and the grated cheese.

4. Slip the pizza from the peel to the very hot stone; if you've used a pizza tray or a baking sheet, place it with the pie in the oven or over the unheated section of the grill. Bake or grill with the lid closed until the cheese has melted and is bubbling and the crust has begun to turn golden brown at its edges, even a darker brown on its underside, 16 to 18 minutes. If working with fresh dough, pop any air bubbles that arise at its edge during the first 10 minutes of baking or grilling.

5. Slide the peel back under the pie to take it off the stone or transfer the pie on its tray or baking sheet to a wire rack. For a crunchier crust, transfer the pie from the peel, tray, or baking sheet right to the wire rack after a minute or so. In any event, cool for 5 minutes before slicing and serving.

Shiitake Pizza

This Asian-inspired pie has a soft, creamy layer of silken tofu spread under the sliced shiitake mushrooms in place of any cheese. Use only the mushroom caps; save the woody, fibrous stems in the freezer in a plastic bag to make vegetable stock. Buy 8 ounces caps and stems to yield about 6 ounces caps.

MAKES 1 PIZZA

All-purpose flour for the pizza peel or nonstick spray for the pizza tray or a
    large baking sheet
One recipe homemade dough, preferably the Classic Pizza Dough (page 23);
    or 1 pound purchased fresh dough or frozen dough, thawed; or one 12- to
    14-inch store-bought, prebaked plain pizza crust
8 ounces (½ pound) soft silken tofu
6 ounces shiitake mushroom caps, stems removed and discarded, caps thinly sliced
3 medium scallions, thinly sliced
2 teaspoons Asian red chile paste
2 teaspoons minced peeled fresh ginger
1 teaspoon regular or reduced-sodium soy sauce
1 teaspoon toasted sesame oil

BAKING OPTIONS

With a pizza stone. Preheat the stone in the oven at 450°F for 30 to 45 minutes; or preheat the stone on a gas grill at medium, indirect heat (about 450°F) for 30 to 45 minutes; or build an indirect, medium-heat coal bed in a charcoal grill and preheat the stone for the same amount of time.

With a pizza tray or a large baking sheet. Preheat the oven to 450°F, a gas grill to indirect, medium heat (about 450°F), or build an indirect, medium-heat coal bed around the edge of a charcoal grill.

CRUST OPTIONS

Fresh dough on a pizza stone. Dust a pizza peel lightly with flour. Set the dough at its center and form the dough into a thick, flat circle by dimpling it with your fingertips. Pick it up, hold it by its edge with both hands, and rotate it, slowly stretching it at the edge, until the circle is about 14 inches in diameter. Set it floured side down on the peel.

Fresh dough on a pizza tray or a large baking sheet. Grease the tray or baking sheet with nonstick spray. Lay the dough on either; dimple the dough with your fingertips—then pull and press it until it forms a 14-inch circle on the tray or an irregular 12 × 7-inch rectangle on the baking sheet.

A prebaked crust. Place it on a pizza peel if using a pizza stone—or place the prebaked crust right on a pizza tray or a large baking sheet.

1. Process the tofu in a food processor fitted with the chopping blade until smooth and creamy. Spread over the prepared crust, making sure you leave a ½-inch border at its edge.

2. Top the tofu with the sliced mushroom caps and scallions. Sprinkle the chile paste, ginger, soy sauce, and sesame oil evenly over the toppings. Slide the pie from the peel to the hot stone or place the pie on its tray or baking sheet either in the oven or over the unheated section of the grill grate.

3. Bake or grill with the lid closed until the crust is golden brown and somewhat firm to the touch, 16 to 18 minutes. Check on fresh dough a few times to make sure there are no air bubbles, particularly at its edge; if so, pop them with a fork to assure an even crust. Once done, slip the peel back under the pie to take it off the hot stone or transfer the pie on its tray or baking sheet to a wire rack. Set aside to cool for 5 minutes before slicing and serving.

Spinach and Ricotta Pizza

Like creamed spinach, that classic steak-house side dish, this topping is a hearty, rich winter warmer. You can make it up to 2 days in advance; store it, covered, in the refrigerator, then reheat in the microwave to spread on the pie.

MAKES 1 PIZZA

Either all-purpose flour for dusting the pizza peel or nonstick spray for greasing the pizza tray or a large baking sheet

One recipe homemade dough, preferably the Classic Pizza Dough (page 23); or 1 pound purchased fresh dough or frozen dough, thawed; or one 12- to 14-inch store-bought, prebaked plain pizza crust

2 tablespoons canola oil

3 garlic cloves, minced

6 ounces baby spinach leaves

¼ teaspoon grated or ground nutmeg

¼ teaspoon red pepper flakes

½ cup dry white wine or dry vermouth

¾ cup regular, low-fat, or fat-free ricotta

1½ ounces Parmigiano-Reggiano, finely grated

½ teaspoon salt

½ teaspoon freshly ground black pepper

BAKING OPTIONS

With a pizza stone. Preheat the stone in the oven at 450°F for 30 to 45 minutes; or preheat the stone on a gas grill at medium, indirect heat (about 450°F) for 30 to 45 minutes; or build an indirect, medium-heat coal bed in a charcoal grill and preheat the stone for the same amount of time.

With a pizza tray or a large baking sheet. Preheat the oven to 450°F, a gas grill to indirect, medium heat (about 450°F), or build an indirect, medium-heat coal bed around the edge of a charcoal grill.

CRUST OPTIONS

Fresh dough on a pizza stone. Dust a pizza peel lightly with flour. Add the dough and form it into a large circle by dimpling it with your fingertips. Pick it up and shape it with your hands, holding its edge, slowly turning the dough and stretching its edge until it's about 14 inches in diameter. Set the dough floured side down on the peel.

Fresh dough on a pizza tray or a large baking sheet. Grease the tray or baking sheet with nonstick spray. Lay the dough on either; dimple the dough with your fingertips until it's a thick, flat circle—then pull and press it until it forms a 14-inch circle on the tray or an irregular 12 × 7-inch rectangle on the baking sheet.

A prebaked crust. Place it on a pizza peel if using a pizza stone—or place the prebaked crust right on a pizza tray or a large baking sheet.

1. Heat a large skillet over medium heat. Swirl in the oil, then add the garlic and cook for 30 seconds.

2. Stir in the spinach, nutmeg, and red pepper flakes just until the leaves begin to wilt; then pour in the wine. Cook, stirring constantly, until the spinach has thoroughly wilted and the skillet is almost dry.

3. Remove the skillet from the heat and stir in the ricotta, grated Parmigiano-Reggiano, salt, and pepper until fairly smooth.

4. Spread the spinach mixture over the prepared crust, leaving a ½-inch border at the edge. Slide the pizza from the peel to the hot stone or place the pizza on its tray or baking sheet either in the oven or over the unheated section of the grill grate.

5. Bake or grill with the lid closed until the filling is set and lightly browned, until the crust is somewhat firm, 16 to 18 minutes. Slide the peel back under the pizza to remove it from the hot stone or transfer the pie on its tray or baking sheet to a wire rack. Set aside to cool for 5 minutes before slicing and serving. To ensure a crunchy crust, transfer the pie from the peel, tray, or baking sheet directly to the wire rack after a couple of minutes.

TEN DEEP-DISH PIZZAS

C all it a Chicago-style pie or a bread pizza, a deep-dish pie is a meal in a pan, a thick layer of cheese and fillings baked in a crust and cut into pie-shaped wedges.

While some deep-dish versions have a top and bottom crust, we prefer a single crust. If there's too much bread, the pie is nothing but a calzone on steroids. We use one crust and line it in a 10-inch cake pan with 2-inch sides. (For a discussion of deep-dish pans, see page 5.) Most of these pies are best when made with a simple crust: the Classic Pizza Dough (page 23). Do not use the various specialty doughs: Spelt, Cracker, or Gluten-Free.

There's one more caveat: use fresh dough, whether homemade or store-bought. There's no way a prebaked crust can be pressed into a deep-dish pan.

Meat Lovers' Deep-Dish Pizza

Look no further for the ultimate indulgence, a pizza layered with four kinds of meats and plenty of cheese. Make sure all the cooked meat is well drained of any juices before adding it to the pie so that the crust doesn't become gummy.

MAKES 1 DEEP-DISH PIZZA

Vegetable oil for greasing the pan

One recipe homemade dough, preferably the Classic Pizza Dough (page 23); or 1 pound purchased fresh dough or frozen dough, thawed

3 ounces pork or turkey bacon strips

6 ounces sweet Italian sausage meat, casings removed

6 ounces lean ground beef

4 ounces mozzarella, shredded

2 ounces pepperoni, thinly sliced

3 tablespoons Classic Pizza Sauce (page 38), No-Cook Pizza Sauce (page 39), or jarred plain pizza sauce

3 tablespoons Pizza Pesto (page 40) or purchased, low-oil pesto

1½ ounces Parmigiano-Reggiano, finely grated

1. Position the rack in the center of the oven and preheat the oven to 450°F. Alternatively, preheat half of a gas grill to 450°F, thereby creating an indirect-heat cooking environment; or make a medium-heat coal bed in a charcoal grill, eventually raking the coals to its outer edge to leave an unheated section of the grate at the center.

2. Lightly grease the inside of a 10-inch cake pan with a little oil dabbed on a paper towel, taking care to get into the seam between the side and bottom. Press the dough into the pan, stretching the dough across the pan's bottom, then pulling the dough a little bit up the sides, about 1 inch. Cover with a clean kitchen towel while you prepare the filling.

3. Place the bacon in a large skillet over medium heat and fry until crisp, turning a couple times, about 4 minutes. Transfer to a plate.

4. Add the sausage and ground beef to the skillet; cook, stirring often, until well browned and cooked through, about 5 minutes. Drain, then set aside.

5. Remove the kitchen towel from over the pan and re-press the dough to create a little 1-inch lip up the inside of the pan. Place the shredded mozzarella in the bottom of the crust, covering it evenly.

6. Top the cheese with the pepperoni, then the browned ground meat and sausage. Finally crumble the bacon evenly over this meat mixture.

7. Dot the pizza sauce and pesto evenly over the pie. Finally, sprinkle evenly with the grated Parmigiano-Reggiano.

8. Place the pan with the pie either in the oven or over the unheated portion of the grill's grate. Bake or grill with the lid closed until the cheese has melted and the sauce is bubbling and a little thick, about 24 minutes. Transfer to a wire rack to cool for 5 to 10 minutes before slicing into thick wedges.

Cheese Lovers' Deep-Dish Pizza

This pie uses both soft ricotta and ricotta salata to create a cheese layer similar to the one in lasagna. But don't worry: there's even more cheese on top! The pie will only be as good as the cheese you use. Search out high-quality ricotta, not made with thickeners or stabilizers, as well as creamy, smooth mozzarella.

MAKES 1 DEEP-DISH PIE

Vegetable oil for greasing the pan

One recipe homemade dough, preferably the Classic Pizza Dough (page 23) or the Semolina Pizza Dough (page 29); or 1 pound purchased fresh dough or frozen dough, thawed

½ cup regular or low-fat ricotta (do not use fat-free)

2½ ounces ricotta salata, finely grated

1 large egg, beaten in a small bowl with a fork until uniform

¼ cup packed, chopped basil leaves

3 ounces mozzarella, shredded

3 ounces Muenster, shredded

⅓ cup Classic Pizza Sauce (page 38), No-Cook Pizza Sauce (page 39), or jarred plain pizza sauce

3½ ounces Provolone, finely grated

1. Position the rack in the center of the oven and preheat the oven to 450°F. Alternatively, preheat half of a gas grill to 450°F, thereby creating an indirect-heat cooking environment; or make a medium-heat coal bed in a charcoal grill, eventually raking the coals to its outer edge to leave an unheated section of the grate at the center.

2. Lightly grease the inside of a 10-inch cake pan with a little oil dabbed on a paper towel. Press the dough into the pan, stretching the dough across the pan's bottom and then pulling the dough a bit up the sides, about 1 inch. Cover with a clean kitchen towel.

3. Mix the ricotta, ricotta salata, egg, and basil in a large bowl until creamy and well blended.

4. Remove the towel and press the dough again so that it forms an edge up the inside of the pan about 1 inch high. Pour the ricotta mixture into the pan and over the dough, spreading the cheese mixture to even it out.

5. Top with the shredded mozzarella and Muenster. Then dot the top of the pie with the pizza sauce, making small dots that will fill in as the pie bakes. Finally, top with the grated Provolone.

6. Place the pie in its pan in the oven or over the unheated section of the grill's grate. Bake or grill with the lid closed until the cheese has melted and the sauce is bubbling and a little thick, about 24 minutes. Transfer to a wire rack to cool for 5 to 10 minutes before slicing into thick wedges.

Mushroom Lovers' Deep-Dish Pizza

Although this recipe calls for cremini mushrooms, feel free to substitute almost any mixture of mushrooms you like, even exotics. However, the cheese will overwhelm the taste of more delicate mushrooms, so save any porcini and chanterelles for other uses. And sliced portobello caps, while bold in flavor, will darken the color of the filling considerably.

MAKES 1 DEEP-DISH PIE

Vegetable oil for greasing the pan
One recipe homemade dough, preferably the Semolina Pizza Dough
  (page 29); or 1 pound purchased fresh dough or frozen dough, thawed
1 tablespoon unsalted butter
10 ounces cremini mushrooms, thinly sliced
1 garlic clove, minced
½ cup dry white wine or dry vermouth
¼ cup chopped chives or the green part of 2 scallions
Up to ½ teaspoon red pepper flakes, optional
¼ teaspoon salt
¼ teaspoon freshly ground black pepper
6 ounces Gruyère, shredded
2½ ounces Parmigiano-Reggiano, finely grated

1. Position the rack in the center of the oven and preheat the oven to 450°F. Alternatively, preheat half of a gas grill to 450°F, thereby creating an indirect-heat cooking environment; or make a medium-heat coal bed in a charcoal grill, eventually raking the coals to its outer edge to leave an unheated section of the grate at the center.

2. Lightly grease the inside of a 10 inch cake pan with a little oil dabbed on a paper towel. Press the dough into the pan, stretching the dough across the pan's bottom and then pulling the dough a little bit up the sides, about 1 inch. Cover with a clean kitchen towel while you prepare the filling.

3. Melt the butter in a large skillet set over medium heat. Add the mushrooms and garlic; cook, stirring often, until the mushrooms begin to give off their liquid and it begins to evaporate, about 5 minutes.

4. Pour in the wine, then let the mixture boil until the liquid in the pan has been reduced to a glaze, about 5 more minutes.

5. Stir in the chives, red pepper flakes (if desired), salt, and pepper. Set aside to cool for 5 minutes.

6. Remove the towel and re-press the dough so that it forms an edge up the inside of the pan about 1 inch high. Sprinkle the shredded Gruyère evenly over the inside of the pie.

7. Top evenly with the sautéed mushroom mixture. Then top with the grated Parmigiano-Reggiano.

8. Set the pie in its pan in the oven or over the unheated section of the grill's grate. Bake or grill with the lid closed until the cheese has melted and the sauce is bubbling and a little thick, about 24 minutes. Transfer to a wire rack to cool for 5 to 10 minutes before slicing into thick wedges.

Ricotta and Sausage Deep-Dish Pizza

This pizza is made with a cheese filling that is topped with cooked sausage and plenty of pizza sauce. Accompany this rich pie with a vinaigrette-dressed green salad.

MAKES 1 DEEP-DISH PIE

Vegetable oil for greasing the pan

One recipe homemade dough, preferably the Classic Pizza Dough (page 23); or 1 pound purchased fresh dough or frozen dough, thawed

8 ounces (½ pound) sweet Italian sausage, casings removed

1 cup regular or low-fat ricotta (do not use fat-free)

4 ounces (¼ pound) mozzarella, shredded

¼ teaspoon grated or ground nutmeg

¼ teaspoon salt

1 large egg, well beaten with a fork in a small bowl

1 cup Classic Pizza Sauce (page 38), No-Cook Pizza Sauce (page 39), or jarred plain pizza sauce

1½ ounces Parmigiano-Reggiano, finely grated

1. Position the rack in the center of the oven and preheat the oven to 450°F. Alternatively, preheat half of a gas grill to 450°F, thereby creating an indirect-heat cooking environment; or make a medium-heat coal bed in a charcoal grill, eventually raking the coals to its outer edge to leave an unheated section of the grate at the center.

2. Lightly grease the inside of a 10-inch cake pan with a little oil dabbed on a paper towel, taking care to get into the seam between the side and bottom. Press the dough into the pan, stretching the dough across the pan's bottom and then pulling the dough a bit up the sides, about 1 inch. Cover with a clean kitchen towel.

3. Crumble the sausage meat into a large skillet set over medium heat. Cook, stirring often, until the sausage is well browned and cooked through, about 4 minutes. Drain and set aside.

4. Mix the ricotta, shredded mozzarella, nutmeg, salt, and the egg in a large bowl until creamy and well blended.

5. Remove the towel and re-press the dough so that it forms an edge up the inside of the pan, about 1 inch high. Pour the ricotta mixture over the dough, spreading the filling with a rubber spatula to even it out.

6. Top with the cooked sausage meat. Then dot evenly all over with the pizza sauce. Finally, top with the grated Parmigiano-Reggiano.

7. Set the filled pan in the oven or over the unheated portion of the grill's grate. Bake or grill with the lid closed until the cheese has melted and the sauce is bubbling and a little thick, about 30 minutes. Transfer to a wire rack to cool for 5 to 10 minutes before slicing into thick wedges.

Chili Deep-Dish Pizza

This thick, hearty pizza is like chili pie in an Italian crust. Both the juice and the tomatoes from a 14-ounce can are used, but at separate points in the recipe, so don't discard the juice when draining the tomatoes.

MAKES 1 DEEP-DISH PIE

One recipe homemade dough, preferably the Classic Pizza Dough (page 23); or 1 pound purchased fresh dough or frozen dough, thawed

1 tablespoon vegetable oil, plus additional for greasing the pan

1 small onion, chopped

½ medium green bell pepper, seeded and chopped

8 ounces (½ pound) lean ground beef

2 tablespoons chili powder

2 teaspoons ground cumin

One 14-ounce can diced tomatoes, the juice and tomatoes reserved separately

3 ounces mozzarella, shredded

3 ounces Cheddar, shredded

3 ounces queso blanco, crumbled

1. Position the rack in the center of the oven and preheat the oven to 450°F. Alternatively, preheat half of a gas grill to 450°F, thereby creating an indirect-heat cooking environment; or make a medium-heat coal bed in a charcoal grill, eventually raking the coals to its outer edge to leave an unheated section of the grate at the center.

2. Lightly grease the inside of a 10-inch cake pan with a little oil dabbed on a paper towel. Press the dough into the pan, stretching the dough across the pan's bottom and then pulling the dough a bit up the sides, about 1 inch. Cover with a clean kitchen towel.

3. Heat the oil in a large skillet set over medium heat. Add the onion and bell pepper; cook, stirring often, until softened, about 3 minutes.

4. Crumble in the ground beef; cook, stirring often, until well browned and cooked through, about 5 minutes.

5. Stir in the chili powder and cumin, then pour in the juice from the canned tomatoes. Cook, stirring constantly, until the liquid in the pan has turned into a thick, glazelike sauce, 2 to 4 minutes. Set aside.

6. Remove the towel and re-press the dough so that it forms an edge up the inside of the pan about 1 inch high. Sprinkle the shredded mozzarella and Cheddar evenly over the inside of the crust.

7. Top with the ground-beef mixture, then sprinkle the canned diced tomatoes evenly over the pizza. Finally, top with the crumbled queso blanco.

8. Set the pie in its pan in the oven or over the unheated section of the grill's grate. Bake or grill with the lid closed until the cheese has melted and the sauce is bubbling and a little thick, about 30 minutes. Transfer to a wire rack to cool for 5 to 10 minutes before slicing into thick wedges.

Barbecue Bacon Cheeseburger Deep-Dish Pizza

This pie is like one of those over-the-top, loaded-to-the-ceiling hamburgers. Use a fairly straightforward barbecue sauce (no fruit bases or Asian spices), so that the sauce doesn't complicate the other flavors in this rich pie.

MAKES 1 DEEP-DISH PIE

Vegetable oil for greasing the pan

One recipe homemade dough, preferably the Classic Pizza Dough (page 23); or 1 pound purchased fresh dough or frozen dough, thawed

6 ounces bacon strips

6 ounces lean ground beef

3 ounces mozzarella, shredded

3 ounces Emmental, Swiss, or Jarlsberg, shredded

½ cup barbecue sauce

2 ounces smoked Cheddar, shredded

1. Position the rack in the center of the oven and preheat the oven to 450°F. Alternatively, preheat half of a gas grill to 450°F, thereby creating an indirect-heat cooking environment; or make a medium-heat coal bed in a charcoal grill, eventually raking the coals to its outer edge to leave an unheated section of the grate at the center.

2. Lightly grease the inside of a 10-inch cake pan with a little oil dabbed on a paper towel, taking care to get into the seam between the side and bottom. Press the dough into the pan, stretching the dough across the pan's bottom and then pulling the dough up the sides, about 1 inch. Cover with a clean kitchen towel while you prepare the filling.

3. Place the bacon strips in a large skillet, then set it over medium heat. Cook, turning two or three times, until crisp and browned, about 4 minutes. Transfer to a plate.

4. Crumble the ground beef into the skillet. Cook in the rendered bacon fat, stirring often, until well browned and cooked through, about 5 minutes. Drain and set aside.

5. Remove the towel and re-press the dough so that it forms an edge up the inside of the pan about 1 inch high. Sprinkle the shredded mozzarella and the Emmental or its substitute over the inside of the dough.

6. Crumble the bacon evenly over the cheese, then top with the browned ground beef. Dot with the barbecue sauce, making small dots that will fill in when baked. Finally, top evenly with the shredded smoked Cheddar.

7. Place the pan in the center of the oven's rack or on the unheated portion of the grill's rack. Bake or grill with the lid closed until the cheese has melted and the sauce is bubbling and a little thick, about 30 minutes. Transfer to a wire rack to cool for 5 to 10 minutes before slicing into thick wedges.

Broccoli and Cheese Deep-Dish Pizza

his pie is reminiscent of broccoli and cheese sauce, that retro side dish. Work in batches over the sink to squeeze the broccoli of all its moisture.

MAKES 1 DEEP-DISH PIE

Vegetable oil for greasing the pan

One recipe homemade dough, preferably the Classic Pizza Dough (page 23); or 1 pound purchased fresh dough or frozen dough, thawed

3 ounces Monterey Jack, shredded

3 ounces mozzarella, shredded

One 10-ounce package frozen chopped broccoli, thawed and squeezed dry

¼ cup diced red onion

½ cup Classic Pizza Sauce (page 38), No-Cook Pizza Sauce (page 39), or jarred plain pizza sauce

1½ ounces Pecorino, finely grated

1. Position the rack in the center of the oven and preheat the oven to 450°F. Alternatively, preheat half of a gas grill to 450°F, thereby creating an indirect-heat cooking environment; or make a medium-heat coal bed in a charcoal grill, eventually raking the coals to its outer edge to leave an unheated section of the grate at the center.

2. Lightly grease the inside of a 10-inch cake pan with a little oil dabbed on a paper towel. Press the dough into the pan, stretching the dough across the pan's bottom and then pulling the dough up the sides about 1 inch.

3. Sprinkle the shredded Monterey Jack and mozzarella evenly over the bottom of the pie. Top with the broccoli and onion, making sure both are evenly distributed across the surface.

4. Dot the pie with the pizza sauce, then top with the grated Pecorino.

5. Set the pan with its filled pie in the center of the oven's rack or over the un-heated portion of the grill's rack. Bake or grill with the lid closed until the cheese has melted and the sauce is bubbling and a little thick, about 25 minutes. Transfer to a wire rack to cool for 5 to 10 minutes before slicing into thick wedges.

Mediterranean Vegetarian
Deep-Dish Pizza

This vegetarian pizza is well stocked with a host of Mediterranean vegetables, herbs, and even sun-dried tomatoes.

MAKES 1 DEEP-DISH PIE

One recipe homemade dough, preferably the Classic Pizza Dough (page 23); or 1 pound purchased fresh dough or frozen dough, thawed

1 tablespoon olive oil, plus additional for greasing the pan

1 small fennel bulb, trimmed of any fronds and chopped

½ small green bell pepper, seeded and chopped (about ½ cup)

¼ cup chopped red onion

2 garlic cloves, minced

2 ounces sun-dried tomatoes (about 12—do not use those packed in oil), thinly sliced

2 tablespoons chopped basil leaves or 1 tablespoon dried basil, crumbled

1 tablespoon chopped oregano leaves or 2 teaspoons dried oregano, crumbled

½ teaspoon freshly ground black pepper

¼ teaspoon salt

2 tablespoons dry white wine or dry vermouth

3 ounces Gruyère, shredded

3 ounces provolone, shredded

3 ounces soft goat cheese, crumbled

1. Position the rack in the center of the oven and preheat the oven to 450°F. Alternatively, preheat half of a gas grill to 450°F, thereby creating an indirect-heat cooking environment; or make a medium-heat coal bed in a charcoal grill, eventually raking the coals to its outer edge to leave an unheated section of the grate at the center.

2. Grease the inside of a 10-inch cake pan with a little olive oil dabbed on a paper towel, taking care to get into the seam between the side and bottom. Press the dough into the pan, stretching the dough across the pan's bottom and then pulling the dough a bit up the sides, about 1 inch. Cover with a clean kitchen towel.

3. Heat a large skillet over medium heat. Swirl in the olive oil, then add the fennel, bell pepper, and onion. Cook, stirring often, until softened, about 4 minutes.

4. Stir in the garlic, cook for 15 seconds; then stir in the sun-dried tomatoes, basil, oregano, pepper, and salt. Cook, stirring constantly, for 1 minute.

5. Pour in the wine and bring to a simmer. Cook until the liquid in the skillet has been reduced to a glaze, about 1 minute. Cool at room temperature for 10 minutes.

6. Remove the towel and re-press the dough so that it forms an edge up the inside of the pan about 1 inch high. Sprinkle the shredded Gruyère and provolone evenly over the pie.

7. Top with the vegetable mixture, spooning it evenly over the cheese. Then top with the goat cheese.

8. Set the pie in its pan in the oven or over the unheated section of the grill's grate. Bake or grill over indirect heat until the cheese has melted and the sauce is bubbling and a little thick, about 28 minutes. Transfer to a wire rack to cool for 5 to 10 minutes before slicing into thick wedges.

Seafood Newburg Deep-Dish Pizza

This deep-dish pie uses shellfish meat to enrich a cream sauce. Use any kind of shellfish you like: scallops, shrimp, frozen and thawed lobster-tail meat, or even crabmeat—or mix and match two or three to your taste.

MAKES 1 DEEP-DISH PIE

Vegetable oil for greasing the pan

One recipe homemade dough, preferably the Classic Pizza Dough (page 23); or 1 pound purchased fresh dough or frozen dough, thawed

1 tablespoon unsalted butter

1 tablespoon all-purpose flour

⅓ cup dry sherry

⅔ cup light cream

½ teaspoon ground or grated nutmeg

½ teaspoon salt

½ teaspoon freshly ground black pepper

6 ounces Gruyère, shredded

8 ounces (½ pound) cooked shellfish meat, including peeled and deveined cooked shrimp, cooked lobster-tail meat, pasteurized lump crabmeat, or quartered scallops

8 ounces (½ pound) frozen chopped broccoli, thawed and squeezed dry in batches over the sink

2 ounces Manchego, finely grated

1. Position the rack in the center of the oven and preheat the oven to 450°F. Alternatively, preheat half of a gas grill to 450°F, thereby creating an indirect-heat cooking environment; or make a medium-heat coal bed in a charcoal grill, eventually raking the coals to its outer edge to leave an unheated section of the grate at the center.

2. Grease the inside of a 10-inch cake pan with a little oil dabbed on a paper towel. Press the dough into the pan, stretching the dough across the pan's bottom and then pulling the dough a little bit up the sides, about 1 inch. Cover with a clean kitchen towel.

3. Melt the butter in a medium skillet set over low heat. Whisk in the flour until a smooth paste forms. Cook for 30 seconds, whisking constantly.

4. Whisk in the sherry in a slow, steady stream until smooth; then whisk in the cream the same way, just until smooth.

5. Whisk in the nutmeg, salt, and pepper. Continue cooking, whisking all the while, just until the mixture begins to bubble and thicken. Set aside.

6. Remove the towel and re-press the dough so that it forms an edge up the inside of the pan about 1 inch high. Spread the shredded Gruyère evenly over the bottom of the pie.

7. Top with the cooked shellfish meat and the broccoli, spreading both evenly over the cheese. Spoon the cream sauce on top, spreading it evenly to the edges. Finally, top with the grated Manchego.

8. Place the pie in its pan in the center of the oven's rack or over the unheated section of the grill's grate. Bake or grill with the lid closed until the cheese has melted and the sauce is bubbling and a little thick, 22 to 24 minutes. Transfer to a wire rack to cool for 5 to 10 minutes before slicing into thick wedges.

Cheddar Mashed Potatoes
Deep-Dish Pizza

Here, cheese-laced mashed potatoes are spooned into a piecrust and baked until hot and luscious. Call it pure heaven.

MAKES 1 DEEP-DISH PIE

Vegetable oil for greasing the pan

One recipe homemade dough, preferably the Classic Pizza Dough (page 23); or 1 pound purchased fresh dough or frozen dough, thawed

1 pound Yukon gold or other yellow-fleshed potatoes, peeled and quartered

1/3 cup heavy, whipping, or light cream (do not use so-called fat-free cream)

1 tablespoon unsalted butter

2 teaspoons Dijon mustard

1/2 teaspoon freshly ground black pepper

1/4 teaspoon salt

5 ounces Cheddar, shredded

3 ounces Monterey Jack, shredded

4 ounces (1/4 pound) pork or turkey bacon strips

1 medium yellow onion, chopped

2 ounces Parmigiano-Reggiano, finely grated

1. Position the rack in the center of the oven and preheat the oven to 450°F. Alternatively, preheat half of a gas grill to 450°F, thereby creating an indirect-heat cooking environment; or make a medium-heat coal bed in a charcoal grill, eventually raking the coals to its outer edge to leave an unheated section of the grate at the center.

2. Lightly grease the inside of a 10-inch cake pan with a little oil dabbed on a paper towel, taking care to get into the seam between the side and bottom. Press the dough into the pan, stretching the dough across the pan's bottom and then pulling the dough up the sides about 1 inch. Cover with a clean kitchen towel while you prepare the filling.

3. Bring about 1 inch water to a boil over high heat in a pot fitted with a vegetable steamer. Add the potatoes, cover, and steam until tender when pierced with a fork, about 15 minutes.

4. Pour the potatoes into a large bowl and mash with the cream, butter, mustard, pepper, and salt. Fold in both the shredded Cheddar and Monterey Jack.

5. Uncover the crust; make sure it still goes about an inch up the inside of the pan. Spread the potato mixture evenly into the crust.

6. Place the bacon in a large skillet over medium heat. Cook, turning a few times, until crispy and browned, about 6 minutes. Transfer the bacon to a plate.

7. Add the onion to the bacon drippings in the skillet. Continue cooking over medium heat, stirring often, until softened, about 3 minutes.

8. Crumble the bacon over the potatoes, then sprinkle the onion and any bacon drippings remaining in the pan over the top. Finally, sprinkle the grated Parmigiano-Reggiano evenly over the pie.

9. Set the pie in its pan in the oven or over the unheated section of the grill's grate. Bake or grill with the lid closed until the cheese has melted and the crust has begun to brown lightly at its edges, about 22 minutes. Transfer to a wire rack to cool for 5 to 10 minutes before slicing into thick wedges.

Acknowledgments

Once again, we thank Harriet Bell, our editor deluxe, who has worked with us to turn this book into what it now is. Her hand is everywhere and the book is better for it.

Thanks, too, to Sarah Whitman-Salkin, who has stewarded the book through Harper. We also can't say enough good things about David Sweeney, the director of the cookbook division, as well as Sonia Greenbaum who copyedited the book, Ann Cahn and Lorie Young who were the production editors, and Alison Forner who designed the cover.

We continue to owe so much to our literary agent, Susan Ginsburg, who has helped us fashion this career out of the shards of old media. And our gratitude, too, to her assistant, Bethany Strout, who seems always able to calm down author's panic.

Thanks to Tom Wanke at Weber for the testosterone-pumping grill on our deck. Thanks, too, to Gretchen Holt at OXO for kitchen gadgets aplenty, and once again, to Melanie Tennant at All-Clad Metalcrafters, this time for pizza wheels and stones.

More pizzas were tasted by Stephanie Thiebault, our dog's patient friend and confidante, than by anyone else. This book reflects the things she likes—and omits some of the pies she left alone.

Finally, thanks to Barbara and Richard Fabian, the owners of Sit-N-Knit in Bloomfield, Connecticut, and the women of the Thursday night knitting group. They tasted pizza after pizza—and made recipe testing so darn enjoyable.

Index

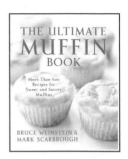

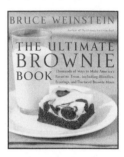   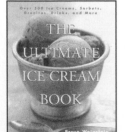